PENGUIN BOOKS — GREAT FOOD

Notes from Madras

COLONEL ARTHUR ROBERT KENNEY-HERBERT ('COLONEL WYVERN') greatly influenced Elizabeth David in her studies of spices in the English kitchen. Wyvern's *Culinary Jottings for Madras* first appeared in 1878 and was written to instruct memsahibs in India on how to produce good Anglo-Indian food in the Victorian style with the ingredients available, and also to instruct mystified native cooks on the English appetite. He returned to Britain to set up a successful cookery school in London.

Notes from Madras

COLONEL WYVERN

PENGUIN BOOKS

PENGUIN BOOKS

Published by the Penguin Group

Penguin Books Ltd, 80 Strand, London WC2R 0RL, England

Penguin Group (USA) Inc., 375 Hudson Street, New York, New York 10014, USA

Penguin Group (Canada), 90 Eglinton Avenue East, Suite 700, Toronto, Ontario,
Canada M4P 2Y3 (a division of Pearson Penguin Canada Inc.)

Penguin Ireland, 25 St Stephen's Green, Dublin 2, Ireland
(a division of Penguin Books Ltd)

Penguin Group (Australia), 250 Camberwell Road,
Camberwell, Victoria 3124, Australia
(a division of Pearson Australia Group Pty Ltd)

Penguin Books India Pvt Ltd, 11 Community Centre,
Panchsheel Park, New Delhi – 110 017, India

Penguin Group (NZ), 67 Apollo Drive, Rosedale, Auckland 0632, New Zealand
(a division of Pearson New Zealand Ltd)

Penguin Books (South Africa) (Pty) Ltd, 24 Sturdee Avenue,
Rosebank, Johannesburg 2196, South Africa

Penguin Books Ltd, Registered Offices: 80 Strand, London WC2R 0RL, England

www.penguin.com

Culinary Jottings for Madras first published 1878
This extract published in Penguin Books 2011
This edition published for The Book People Ltd, 2011
Hall Wood Avenue, Haydock, St Helens, WA11 9UL

1

Set in 10.75/13pt Berkeley Oldstyle Book
Typeset by Jouve (UK), Milton Keynes
Printed in Great Britain by Clays Ltd, St Ives plc

Cover design based on a plate from Bombay, *c.* 1880. Glazed earthenware.
(Photograph copyright © Victoria & Albert Museum.) Picture research
by Samantha Johnson. Lettering by Stephen Raw

ISBN 978–0–241–96076–9

www.greenpenguin.co.uk

Contents

In the Store-room   1

Our Curries   7

Curries – continued, and Mulligatunny   21

Camp Cookery   39

On Coffee-Making   57

Our Kitchens in India   60

In the Store-room

On visiting the vast collections of tinned provisions, sauces, &c., at some of the large establishments at the Presidency, I have often wondered how a lady, commencing house-keeping, is guided in selecting the things she requires for her store-room. A majority, no doubt, of the fair *châtelaines* of Madras, do their shopping at their boudoir writing tables, filling up lists at the dictation of the butler at their elbow; for few, I take it, – very few care to go to the fountain head for what they want.

Now, a butler's ideas about stores are, on the whole, very mixed: he worships 'Europe articles' and delights in filling the shelves of the store-room with rows of tins; of which some may perhaps be useful, but many need never be bought at all at Madras, and so remain for months untouched, lumbering the shelves of the cupboard. It has struck me, therefore, that a few words regarding the choosing of stores may be acceptable.

I have long come to the conclusion that the fewer accessories you use in the way of hermetically sealed provisions in the cooking of a dinner the better. In Madras we have all the materials for soup-making at hand, we have excellent fish, very fair flesh and fowl, good wild fowl and game when in season, and vegetables from Bangalore and the Neilgherries in addition to the standard produce of the country. If, therefore, we concentrate our attention sufficiently upon what we can get from market, our demand on tinned food should be very small indeed.

Take now, for instance, a tin of the ordinary preserved mushrooms, – those made you know of white leather, – what is the use of them, what do they taste of? Yet people giving a dinner party frequently garnish one *entrée* at least with them, and the Madras butler would be horrified if his mistress were to refuse him that pleasure. The stewed 'black Leicestershire' are the best preserved mushrooms to be had, but even between them and the fresh fungus, there is a great gulf fixed.

A few years ago I met an officer of the Artillery, who, after having served in various parts of the world, had just been appointed to a command in this Presidency. Conversation happened to turn upon cookery, and the Colonel soon proved himself to be a man who had for years studied the science *con amore*. He had had little or no experience of Indian life, and he expressed himself agreeably surprised, rather than otherwise, at the style of living to which he had been introduced. 'But,' he said, 'preserve me from your dinners of ceremony.' He had arrived, he told me, quite unexpectedly a few evenings before, and had been at once invited to the Mess; the dinner, – just the ordinary daily one, – was, he thought, excellent, and so it was the next day, and the day following, but on the fourth day he was formally invited to dine as a Mess guest, and that was a very different affair. Considerable expense had been incurred, he observed, on this occasion in tinned provisions, but with the worst possible result. There was a dish of preserved salmon *hot*, and sodden; the *entrées* were spoilt by the introduction of terrible sausages, and mushrooms; and the tinned vegetables were ruined by being wrongly treated by the cook. 'There are few men,' the Colonel went on, 'who have had more to do with preserved provisions than I have, but until I attended this big Indian dinner, I never saw such things actually regarded as delicacies, and put upon the table to the exclusion of the good fresh food procurable in the market.' This is the proper way of looking at this question. There will be times and places, when and where you will be obliged to fall back upon Messrs. Crosse and Blackwell, and be thankful. Until those evil days come upon you, however, do not anticipate your penance, but strive to make the food you can easily procure, palatable and good by scientific treatment.

I look upon tinned provisions in the hands of Ramasámy as the cloaks of carelessness, and slovenly cooking. He thinks that the 'tin' will cover a multitude of sins, so takes comparatively little pains with the dish that it accompanies.

There are many ladies who, when giving out stores for a dinner party, have no hesitation in issuing 'tins' to the value of many rupees, but if asked for extra cream, butter, eggs, and gravy-meat, – the true essentials of cookery, – begin to consider themselves imposed upon. The poverty of our cookery in India results almost wholly from our habit of ignoring these things, the very backbone, as it were, of the cook's art. If an English cook, surrounded with the best market supplies in the world, be helpless without her stock, her kitchen butter, and her cream and eggs, how much more should Ramasámy be pitied if he be refused those necessaries, for his materials stand in far greater need of assistance.

In the matter of firewood and charcoal too, I am aware that there is often a difference of opinion between the cook and his mistress, and I am inclined to think that Ramasámy is generally in the wrong. Still, we should be careful lest we limit his supply of fuel too closely – especially on a dinner party day. I once was a guest at a house where the dinner was served perfectly as far as the joint, when a sudden collapse took place; the game and dressed vegetable were stone-cold. The excuse the next day was, 'charcoal all done finish, and Missis only got godown key in the pocket.'

Unless you have tried to find out practically what can be done with the fish, flesh, fowl, and vegetables of this country, by studious cookery, you will scarcely believe the extent of your power, and how independent you really are of preserved provisions. It is absolutely annoying to read the nonsense people write about our style of living in India. I remember an article headed 'Curry and Rice' which once appeared in *Vanity Fair*. The writer wrecked on the rock upon which many drift, who, with a little knowledge of the peculiarities of some particular part of the country, sit down with impudent confidence to treat of India generally, quite forgetting that the Peninsula is a large one, and that the manners and customs which obtain in one district, may never have been heard of in other parts of the Empire. The article was not applicable to any part of the Madras Presidency, and judging from the writer's suggestions as to the cookery of a tin of beef with yams, and worse still, the fabrication of soup *from the fowl bones you picked and left at luncheon*, I should say that *Vanity* had picked up not only an ignoramus, but an uncleanly ignoramus, as a contributor. Our friends at Home were told by this audacious man that no dinner was complete in India without a 'burning curry,' and that none was successful 'without Europe tins.' I think that, as we go on, I shall be able to prove that at Madras, at all events, we can do pretty well without either.

Although I am strongly against the use of tinned things to the extent that many allow, there are nevertheless many articles which you *must* have in the store-room: – pickles, sauces, jams, bacon, cheese, maccaroni, vermicelli, vinegars, flavouring essences, the invaluable truffle, tart fruits, biscuits, isinglass, arrowroot, oatmeal, pearl barley, cornflour, olives, capers, dried herbs, and so on. Grated Parmesan cheese (sold in bottles by Crosse and Blackwell) should never be forgotten, the salad oil should be the best procurable, and no store-room should be without tarragon vinegar, anchovy vinegar, French vinegar, and white wine vinegar. Amongst sauces I consider 'Harvey' the best for general use; Sutton's 'Empress of India,' is a strong sauce with a real flavour of mushrooms; Moir's sauces and 'Reading sauce' are very trustworthy, and there are others which, no doubt, commend themselves to different palates, but I denounce 'Worcester sauce' and 'Tapp's sauce' as agents far too powerful to be trusted to the hands of the native cook. Sutton's essence of anchovies is said to possess the charm of not clotting, or forming a stoppage in the neck of the bottle. I have a deep respect for both walnut and mushroom ketchup, soy, and tomato conserve. Then as special trifles, we must not forget caviare, *olives farcies*, and anchovies in oil.

The cook should be carefully shown the use of flavouring essences, and also that of dried herbs. He ought also to be taught never to run out of bread crumbs. Stale fine crumbs should be made every now and then, and kept corked down in bottles for use when required. The very unsightly appearance presented by fish, cutlets, etc., crumbed with fresh spongy crumbs should warn us, for stale bread is never to be had when we suddenly want it. Red currant jelly is very useful; the store-room should never be 'out' of it. *Macèdoines*, *fonds d'artichaut*, *petits pois*, *haricots verts* and *asperges* are, of course, excellent, and the dried *Julienne* will be found admirable for soups. Preserved fish is not required at Madras, and we can get on without tinned meats, soups, and potted luxuries; for we can make better things at home.

In sweet things, however, we are not so independent, and jams, jellies, tart-fruits, dried and candied peel, currants, raisins, ginger, &c., &c., must all have room in the house-keeper's cupboard.

Our Curries

We are often told by men of old time, whose long connection with the country entitles them to speak with the confidence of 'fellows who know, don't you know,' that in inverse proportion, as it were, to the steady advance of civilization in India, the sublime art of curry-making has gradually passed away from the native cook. Elders at Madras – erst-while the acknowledged head-centre of the craft – shake their heads and say 'Ichabod!' and if encouraged to do so, paint beautiful mouth-watering 'pictures in words' of succulent morsels cunningly dressed with all the savoury spices and condiments of Ind, the like of which, they say, we ne'er shall look upon again.

Looking back myself to the hour of my arrival in India, I call to mind the kind-hearted veteran who threw his doors open to me, and, pouring in the oil and wine of lavish hospitality, set me upon his own beast, killed the fatted calf, and treated me, indeed, as a son that had been lost and was found. It rejoiced this fine old servant of honest John Company, I remember, to give 'tiffin' parties at which he prided himself on sending round eight or nine varieties of curries, with divers platters of freshly-made chutneys, grilled ham, preserved roes of fishes, &c. The discussion of the 'course,' – a little banquet in itself – used to occupy at least half an hour, for it was the correct thing to taste each curry, and to call for those that specially gratified you a second time.

Now, this my friend was, I take it, a type of the last Anglo-Indian generation; a generation that fostered the art of curry-making, and bestowed as much attention to it as we, in these days of grace, do to copying the culinary triumphs of the lively Gauls.

Thirty years ago fair house-keepers were wont to vaunt themselves upon their home-made curry powders, their chutneys, tamarind and roselle jellies, and so forth, and carefully superintended the making thereof. But fashion has changed, and although ladies are, I think, quite as fond of a good curry as their grandmothers were, they rarely take the trouble to gather round them the elements of success, and have ceased to be cumbered about this particular branch of their cook's work.

This is an important point, for if we enquire closely into the causes that have led to the alleged decay of the curry-making knack, we shall certainly find that the chief of them is want of care in the preparation of powders and pastes, and the loss of recipes which in days gone by were wrapped in silver paper, and preserved with miniatures painted on ivory, locks of hair, love sonnets, and other precious secrets of a lady's escritoire.

I say 'chief' advisedly, for there can be no doubt that modern improvements in our *cuisine*, and modern good taste, have assisted in a measure in elbowing off the once delectable *plats* of Indian origin; and that the best curry in the world would never be permitted to appear at a *petit-dîner* composed by a good disciple of the new *régime*.

Curries now-a-days are only licensed to be eaten at breakfast, at luncheon, and perhaps at the little home dinner, when they may, for a change, occasionally form the *pièce de résistance* of that cosy meal. Having thus lost 'caste,' so to speak, it ought hardly to surprise us that curries have deteriorated in quality. The old cooks, who studied the art, and were encouraged in its cultivation, have passed away to their happy hunting grounds; and the sons and grandsons who now reign in their stead have been taught to devote themselves to more fashionable dishes.

While, however, it cannot be denied that the banishment of curries from the *menu* of our high-art banquets, both great and small, is, for many reasons, indispensably necessary, there can be no doubt that at mess and club dinners, at hotels, and at private houses, as already shown, these time-honoured dishes will always be welcome. Has not the time arrived then for us to endeavour to resuscitate the ancient cunning of our cooks, and to take some pains to attain that end?

The actual cooking of a curry presents no special difficulty. A cook who is an adept with the stew-pan, and who has mastered the art of slow, and very gentle simmering, will, whether a Frenchman, an Englishman, or a mild Hindu, soon become familiar with the treatment of this particular dish.

The knotty points are these: – First the powder or paste, next the accessories, and lastly the order in which the various component parts should be added.

Concerning powders, it behoves us to proceed with caution, or we shall soon lose ourselves in a maze of recipes. Speaking of them generally, however, it is not, I think, commonly known that curry-powders improve by keeping it carefully bottled. One of the causes of our daily failures is undoubtedly the lazy habit we have adopted of permitting our cooks to fabricate their 'curry-stuff,' on the spot, as it is required. Powder should be made in large quantities under the eye of the mistress of the house, or that of a really trustworthy head-servant. It should then be bottled, and corked securely down.

I shall presently give a very valuable receipt for a stock household powder, one that was surrendered to me by an accomplished *châtelaine*, on the eve of her departure from India, as a token of the sincerest friendship. But for those who wish to avoid trouble and yet to have good curries, I strongly advocate the use of Barrie's Madras curry-powder and paste. I am not employed as an advertising medium. My advice is not the advice of a 'gent' travelling for Messrs. Barrie and Co., it is the honest exhortation of one, my friends, who has the success of your curries very closely at heart.

After more than twenty years' experience of Barrie's condiments, I say boldly, that I am aware of no preparations in the market that can equal them. At the 'Oriental Depôt,' on the southern side of Leicester Square, – a sanctuary known, I fear, to too few Anglo-Indians at home – you can see, or *could* see, (for the little place may have been swept away for aught I know with Northumberland House, Temple Bar and other structures of renown), sundry casks of Barrie's curry-stuffs, chutneys, &c. I discovered the place by a mere accident, and the smell and the order-book convinced me that I had not made a mistake. The former was that of my friend Barrie, and the latter contained names of such high degree in connection with India that I immediately removed my hat.

Unfortunately the depôt is largely patronized by London grocers, who, over-wise in their generation, use the condiments they purchase as mere stock wherewith to flavour some miserable concoction of their own manufacture. Two parts of arrowroot coloured with saffron, and one part of Barrie, for instance, is a mixture that can hardly with justice be called 'genuine Madras curry-powder,' notwithstanding its being bottled in a very pretty bottle, and priced two and six.

I detected the presence of Barrie's excellent *mulligatunny* paste at several places at home, especially at Mutton's at Brighton, where a basin of the *potage Indien* for lunch on a frosty day used to be a thing worth recording in a pilgrim's diary with red letters.

Assuming that we have procured, or made, a really good stock powder, the accessories next present themselves for our consideration. These are very important, for, with their aid, a clever cook can diversify the flavour, and style of his curries; without them – be the powder or paste never so well composed – the dish will certainly lack finish, and the true characteristics of a good curry.

Prominently among them stands the medium to be

used for the frying of the onions, with which the process commences. This most assuredly should be butter. The quantity required is not very great, and surely it may be assumed that people who want to have a good curry will not ruin it for the sake of a 'two ounce pat of Dosset!' for be it noted, that tinned butter of a good brand is admirably adapted for this work.

Among other adjuncts that may be written down as indispensable are the ingredients needed to produce that suspicion of sweet-acid which it will be remembered, forms a salient feature of a superior curry. The natives of the south use a rough tamarind conserve worked, sometimes, with a very little jaggery or molasses, and a careful preparation of tamarind is decidedly valuable. Why, however, should we not improve upon this with red currant jelly, and if further sharpness be needed, a little lime or lemon juice? In England, and I daresay in India also, chopped apple is sometimes used, and perhaps chopped mango, in the fool-days of the fruit, would be nice. A spoonful of sweetish chutney and a little vinegar or lime juice can be employed, but I confess that I prefer the red currant jelly as aforesaid.

There are also certain green leaves which are undoubtedly not to be despised as flavouring agents. By their means flavours can be effectively changed. I will speak of them again when discussing the process of curry-making step by step.

Then there is that most important item the cocoanut. This, as everyone knows, is added to a curry in the form of 'milk,' *i.e.*, an infusion produced by scraping the white nutty part of the cocoanut, and soaking the scrapings in boiling water. This, strained, is the 'milk' required in curry-making. The quantity to be used depends upon the nature of the curry. Malay curries, for instance, require a great deal of 'milk.' The point in connection with this adjunct, however, that must not be missed, is the period at which it should be added. If put in too soon, the value of the nutty juice will be lost, – cooked away, and overpowered by the spicy condiments with which it is associated. So we must reserve the 'milk,' as we do cream or the yolk of an egg in the case of a thick soup or rich sauce, and stir it into our curry the last thing just before serving.

The strained milk extracted from pounded sweet almonds can be put into a curry very advantageously: it may be used alone, or be associated with cocoanut milk. One ounce of the latter, to twelve almonds, will be found a pleasant proportion. When cocoanuts cannot be got, almond milk makes a capital substitute.

Curries cannot afford to dispense with the assistance of some stock or gravy. It is not uncommon to hear people say that they have eaten far better curries in England than in India, the chief reason being that Mary Jane will not undertake to make the dish without at least a breakfast-cupful and a half of good stock.

Let us now consider attentively the actual details of curry-making, and since we cannot proceed to work without a good powder or paste, we can hardly do better than commence operations by studying the recipe for a household curry-stuff, concerning which I have already spoken. If faithfully followed, it will, I am sure, be found most trustworthy. It runs as follows: –

4 lbs.	of turmeric ...	...	Hind.	*huldi.*
8 lbs.	of coriander-seed	...	"	*dhunnia.*
2 lbs.	of cummin-seed	...	"	*jeera.*
1 lb.	of poppy-seed ...	...	"	*khush-khush.*
2 lbs.	of fenugreek ...	...	"	*maythi.*
1 lb.	of dry-ginger ...	...	"	*sont.*
½ lb.	of mustard-seed	...	"	*rai.*
1 lb.	of dried chillies	...	"	*sooka mirrch.*
1 lb.	of black pepper corns.		"	*kala mirrch.*

Do not be alarmed at the quantity, remembering my previous statement that curry-powder *improves* by keeping, if carefully secured. The amount when finally mixed will fill about half a dozen bottles of the size in which tart fruits are imported. Accordingly, if disinclined to lay in so large a stock at a time, the obvious alternative of sharing some of it with a friend can easily be adopted.

The lady who gave me the receipt accompanied her kind action with a little good advice: – 'Weigh everything,' said she, 'most carefully, and even after the various ingredients have been cleaned, weigh them again, and also weigh the husks, &c., that have been removed. In this way alone will you be able to guard against the disappearance of half an ounce of this, or an ounce of that, – petty pilferings that take from the curry-powder that which it cannot get again, and leave it poor indeed.'

Inasmuch, therefore, as short weight can be more easily detected in fairly large than in small quantities, an additional reason presents itself for making up the entire recipe.

The coriander-seed and fenugreek must each be parched very carefully, *i.e.*, roasted like coffee berries, before being pounded, and the other ingredients should be cleaned and dried, each separately, and, when pounded, should be well sifted.

In order to preserve the proportions after the seeds have been powdered and sifted, it is necessary to obtain much larger quantities of the various ingredients in the first instance. Coriander-seed, for example, is very oily and only a part of it will pass through the sieve; twenty-four ounces of the seed will not yield more than eight ounces of powder: eight ounces of turmeric root will give four of powder: cummin-seed loses about one-third of its original weight in the process of sifting, and dried chilli skin about half.

Weights having been tested, then the whole of the powders should be mixed, a quarter of a bottle of salt being sprinkled in by degrees during the process. The bottles, thoroughly cleansed and dried in the sun, may now be filled and corked tightly down, the tops being securely waxed over.

Some recommend that, when the powder has been mixed, it should be browned in melted butter over the fire, then dried in the sun, and powdered again, in order to tone down the strong flavour of the cummin-seed.

This is a *stock* powder, the flavour of which can be varied by the use of certain spices, and green leaves, garlic, onions, green ginger, almond, cocoanut, &c., at the time of cooking the curry.

The spices, which should be used according to taste and discretion, are these: – cloves (*laoong*), mace (*jawatri*), cinnamon (*kulmi darchini*), nutmeg (*jaephal*), cardamoms (*eelachi*), and allspice (*seetul chini gach*). A salt-spoonful of one, or at most of two, of these aromatic powders blended, will suffice for a large curry. Dr. Kitchener's precept, *viz.*, that the mixing of several spices is a blunder, should never be forgotten.

The green leaves that are often useful when judiciously introduced are: – fennel (*souf*), 'maythi bajee,' lemon-grass (*uggea-ghas*), bay-leaves (*tajipatha*), 'karaypauk,' 'kotemear' leaves (green coriander), &c.

When green ginger is used it should be sliced very fine, and pounded to a paste; a dessert-spoonful being sufficient for one curry.

The indispensably necessary suspicion of sweet-acid can be produced most readily by a dessert-spoonful of powdered or moist sugar and the juice of a lime, or a spoonful of vinegar. A table-spoonful of sweet chutney and the juice of a lime make a good substitute; but a table-spoonful of red currant jelly, with one of chutney, and a little vinegar or lime juice, form to my mind the nicest combination for *dark* curries.

I strongly advocate the very capital plan of making a fresh paste of some of the above adjuncts, in sufficient quantity for the curry in hand, and blending it with the stock powder when cooking the latter. Here is a reliable recipe: – One small onion, one clove of garlic, one dessert-spoonful of turmeric, one of freshly-roasted coriander-seed, one of poppy-seed, a tea-spoonful of Nepaul pepper, one of sugar, one of salt, and one of grated green ginger.

Pound all these with sufficient good salad oil to make a paste. Also pound twelve almonds, and one ounce of cocoanut, with a little lime juice to assist the operation. Then mix the two pastes, and stir into them a salt-spoonful of cinnamon or clove-powder. A heaped up table-spoonful of this paste to one of the stock powder will produce a very excellent result. Additional heat can be obtained by those who like very hot curries if red chilli powder be added to the above ingredients accord-ing to taste. This paste will keep if put away carefully and covered up.

Having satisfied ourselves as to the composition of our powder and paste, we may now work out, step by step, the process to be followed in cooking a chicken curry.

Choose a nice young chicken – and here let me point out that *large* chickens nearly full grown ought never to be used in curries – and having cut it up neatly as for a *fricassée*, place the pieces aside, and dredge over them a little flour. Next take all the trimmings, neck, pinions, leg bones, feet, head, &c., with any scraps of meat that can be spared, and cast them into a sauce-pan with an onion sliced, a carrot sliced, half a dozen pepper corns, a bit of celery, a pinch of salt and one of sugar, cover them with cold water and make the best broth you can. When ready, strain the contents of the sauce-pan into a bowl, and skim it clean. A good breakfast-cupful of weak stock should thus be obtained. Lastly, make a breakfast-cupful of milk of cocoanut, or almond.

Now take your stew-pan, and having sliced up six good shallots, or two small white onions, cast the rings into it, with two ounces of Denmark, Normandy, or other good tinned butter; add a finely-minced clove of garlic, and fry till the onions turn a nice yellow brown. Then add a heaped-up table-spoonful of the stock powder, and one of the paste, or, if you have not made the latter, two table-spoonfuls of the powder. Cook the curry-stuff with the onions and butter for a minute or two, slowly, adding by degrees a wine-glassful of the cocoanut milk, and then also by degrees the breakfast-cupful of broth. The effect of this when simmered for a quarter of an hour will be a rich, thick, curry gravy, or sauce. The stew-pan should now be placed *en bain-marie* while we proceed to prepare the chicken.

Take a frying-pan: melt in it an ounce of butter, or clarified beef suet, add a shallot cut up small, and fry for a couple of minutes. Next put the pieces of chicken into the *sauté*-pan, and lightly fry them. As soon as slightly coloured, the pieces of chicken should be transferred to the stew-pan in which they should rest for at least half an hour, marinading, as it were, in the curry gravy. After that, the stew-pan should be placed over a gentle fire, and if the liquid be found insufficient to cover the pieces of chicken, stock, if available, or water, should be added. A gentle simmering process should now be encouraged, during which the bay-leaf, chutney, and sweet-acid should be added. If powder without fresh paste has been used, the pounded almond and cocoanut must now be put in, with a little spice and grated green ginger. The curry gravy should at this period be tasted, and if a little more acid or sweet be found necessary, the proper correction should be made. As soon as the pieces of chicken have become tender, thoroughly stewed, that is to say, a coffee-cupful of cocoanut 'milk,' (the infusion I previously mentioned), should be stirred in, and in three minutes the operation will be complete.

If a semi-dry or dry curry be required, the gravy must be still further reduced by simmering with the lid off, the pieces of meat being continually stirred about with a wooden spoon to prevent their catching at the bottom of the pan. When the proper amount of absorption has been attained, remove the pan and serve.

Now, those to whom the slipshod method of curry-making, ordinarily followed by native cooks, is familiar, will, perhaps, think, that the process I have recommended is needlessly troublesome. The separate frying of the chicken, the period of rest in the *bain-marie*, &c., may seem to them unnecessary. I am, however, perfectly confident that in order to produce a dish of a superior class, we must be prepared to take all this trouble, bringing an enlightened system of cookery to bear upon the condiments and ingredients which, so to speak, provide the curry flavour. I look upon a chicken curry as a *fricassée*, or *blanquette à l'Indienne*, and consider that it should certainly be treated according to the principles of scientific cookery.

The soaking of meat in the liquid curry-stuff is an important point, especially when previously cooked meat is to be curried. Remember how much better a *salmis* or a hash tastes if the meat of which it is composed has been marinaded for an hour or so, before being finally heated up, in the carefully-made gravy or sauce composed for it.

This, I think, accounts for an opinion I once heard expressed by a friend of undoubted ability in culinary criticism, to the effect that he always found curries of a certain kind better when warmed up and served as a *rechauffé* than when presented for the first time. If a gravy curry be kept during the night in a china curry dish, and be resuscitated the next morning with some fresh butter, onions and a little gravy, it ought, if anything, to be found better than on the previous night, since the meat has become thoroughly flavoured by the curry gravy, while the latter has become reduced and so strengthened by the second simmering.

These directions will be found practicable with most ordinary meat curries. Those made of fresh fish, prawns, and shellfish, require a somewhat different process while those of minced cooked meat, tinned or cooked fish, dressed vegetables, and hard-boiled eggs, merely require to be gently heated up in a carefully made curry gravy.

The Malay or 'Ceylon curry' as it is sometimes called, is, of course, a *spécialité* and there are *kubábs*, *quoormas*, &c., &c., that need separate consideration.

Curries – continued,
and Mulligatunny

The outward bound passenger to India is generally very favourably struck by the curry presented to him at a Ceylon hostelry. Heartily weary of the *cuisine* on board ship, at that period of his voyage, he would probably welcome any change with thankfulness. The prospect of a little meal ashore, 'be it ever so humble,' is therefore especially enjoyable to him. It may, of course, be said that in such circumstances the traveller is predisposed to deliver a kindly verdict; and that if the dish that pleased him so much in the hour of his emancipation from cuddy barbarisms were placed before him after a proper course of civilized diet, it would, by no means produce such an agreeable impression. It would, at all events, lack the charm of contrast, which, in the particular instance before us, could hardly fail to excite the warmest feelings of gratitude and satisfaction.

The nautical curry is not, as a rule, a *plat* to dream of, – a triumph to look back upon pleasurably, that is to say, with the half-closed eye of a *connoisseur*. A sea-faring friend with whom I once made a very cheery voyage, graphically described the composition as 'yellow Irish stew.' Those whose memory is retentive of trifles will no doubt call to mind without difficulty a bright saffron-tinted swill, covering sundry knotty lumps of potato and a few bony atoms of mutton, with its surface beflecked, if I may so describe it, with glossy discs of molten grease. Not exactly the sort of dish to tempt a lady, still slightly affected by *mal-de-mer*, who has been urged by her stewardess to rouse herself, 'poor dear,' and try and eat something. Having had this mess thrust before him day after day for three weeks, no wonder that the '*vacuus viator*' finds something in the curry of Ceylon to delight him.

'Good! said I to myself, cheered at the sight' (a plump, freshly-roasted leveret), wrote Brillat Savarin concerning his experiences of a journey; 'I am not entirely abandoned by Providence: *a traveller may gather a flower by the way-side.*'

Regarding the Ceylon curry, then, as a 'flower by the way-side,' let us proceed to consider its composition with all due attention. As I observed in my last chapter, the dish is quite a *spécialité*, peculiar originally to places where the cocoanut is extensively grown and appreciated. It is known by some as the 'Malay curry,' and it is closely allied to the *moli* of the Tamils of Southern India. Though best adapted for the treatment of shell-fish, ordinary fish, and vegetables of the *cucumis* or gourd family, it may be advantageously tried with chicken, or any nice white meat. We can describe it as a species of *fricassée*, rich with the nutty juice of the cocoanut, and very delicately flavoured with certain mild condiments. It ought to be by no means peppery or hot, though thin strips of red and green chilli-skin or capsicum may be associated with it. It therefore possesses characteristics very different from those of an ordinary curry. The knotty point is the treatment and application of the cocoanut, which should be as fresh and juicy as possible, and of which there should be no stint.

In places where cocoanuts cannot be readily procured, a very good 'mock' Ceylon curry can be made with the milk of almonds, and from Brazil nuts an infusion can be concocted that very much resembles cocoanut milk.

The condiments employed are onions, a very little garlic, green ginger, turmeric powder, a little powdered cinnamon and cloves, and the chilli strips aforesaid. Coriander-seed, cummin-seed, cardamoms, fenugreek, chilli-powder, poppy-seed, &c., ought, on no account, to be used.

The most agreeable combinations are prawns with cucumber, crab with vegetable marrow, or any firm-fleshed fish or tender chicken with either of those vegetables. For example, I will select a prawn and cucumber curry: –

(*a*) – Take a good-sized cucumber, or two small ones, cut them lengthwise into quarters, remove the seeds, and peel off the green skin. Cut them into pieces two inches long and one inch thick, and put them into a stew-pan with plenty of water, half an ounce of butter, and a tea-spoonful of salt. Simmer them until three parts done; then drain the liquid off, and turn the pieces of cucumber out upon a clean dish, and cover them up.

(*b*) – The prawns should be prepared very carefully; and here permit me to observe that if prawns are fresh, and *properly cleaned*, no evil effects need be dreaded by those who look upon them as dangerous. Throw two table-spoonfuls of salt into a gallon of water, put the pan on the fire, and when the water boils fast, slip into it

23

about a pound and a half of prawns weighed in their shells. Boil, and as soon as the prawns turn a rosy pink, stop, drain them from the water, let them get cold, and shell them, removing their heads completely. Next pass a knife down the line of the back of each prawn, slightly open the groove as it were, and pick out of it the black gritty dirt that you will find there. Carry out a similar process with the inner line, and cast the cleaned prawns into a basin of spring water. Having washed them again thoroughly, pick them out, and dry them on a cloth. If very large, you must now divide them in halves lengthwise, and sever each half in twain. Dust them over with flour, and put them on a dish. They are now ready.

(*c*) – Choose a very large cocoanut, the fresher the better, break it in half, and, with a cocoanut scraper, remove the whole of the white flesh, casting it into a bowl. Upon the raspings thus obtained, pour a breakfast-cupful of boiling water, leave it for a quarter of an hour, and then strain the liquid off. This is the best or '*number one*' infusion, which must be put away, and not added to the curry till the last thing before serving. Return the raspings to their bowl, and pour over them a pint and a half of boiling water, stir well, and let the liquid stand for half an hour. It should then be strained, and the nutty atoms squeezed dry in muslin, so that every drop of the cocoanut essence may be secured. The liquor thus obtained is the '*number two*' infusion. Our preparations are now complete.

(*d*) – Put two ounces of good tinned butter into a stew-pan, and mix into it, as it melts over a brisk fire, a white Bombay onion shred into rings, and a clove of

24

garlic finely minced. Lightly fry, but do not allow the onions to turn colour before adding a table-spoonful of good flour, a dessert-spoonful of turmeric powder, a tea-spoonful of salt, and a scant one of sugar, a tea-spoonful of mixed cloves and cinnamon powder, and, by degrees, the 'number two infusion.' A breakfast-cupful of thick chicken broth, or fish *consommé* – made by simmering some fish bones, prawn shells, and scraps of fish, in water, with an onion, a carrot, and some parsley – may now go in to assist the composition, together with a heaped-up table-spoonful of sliced green ginger, and three green chillies cut into *Julienne*-like strips. The liquid is now ready for the prawns, so remove the stew-pan from the fire, and place it in a bath of boiling water, to keep warm, while you add the prawns and the slices of partly-cooked cucumber. It will be found an excellent plan to permit the curry – now all but ready – to rest for about half an hour, at the expiration of which the pan may be placed over a moderate fire, and its contents brought to simmering point. When satisfied that both the prawns and vegetable are tender, the 'number one' infusion may be stirred in, and with it a tea-spoonful of lime-juice. Five minutes' simmering will now complete our task, and the curry can be dished up, and served.

It should be noted carefully that the water found inside a cocoanut is not 'cocoanut milk' according to the culinary vocabulary. The *infusion* is what should be used in curry-making.

Fillets of any firm-fleshed fish, or even neat fillets of chicken, may be treated precisely in the manner I have described. As, however, it is necessary partly to cook prawns, crabs, lobsters, shrimps, &c., separately, a longer process of simmering will be necessary for raw fillets. The pieces of chicken should be lightly tossed in butter in a *sauté*-pan with a finely-shred onion, before being put into the curry sauce.

The MOLI is prepared in this manner: – Melt a couple of ounces of butter, and fry therein an onion sliced into rings, and a clove of garlic minced, a few strips of green chilli, and some slices of green ginger; stir into it a table-spoonful of flour, and add by degrees the 'number two infusion' just alluded to. Work this to the consistency of a rich white sauce adding a little broth if necessary, heat up some slices of cooked fish or chicken in it, and finish off, as already described, with 'number one infusion,' and a tea-spoonful of lime-juice. A little turmeric powder may be used if the yellow colour be considered desirable. If raw fish be used, the simmering process will be necessary.

Old Indian cookery books give a number of recipes for KUBÁB curries, for the most part of purely native design, and requiring condiments and ingredients which were perhaps appreciated by our forefathers who adopted an almost Oriental method of life. The best *kubáb*, to my mind, is one made of tender mutton or veal, and treated as follows: –

Cut the mutton into thickish pieces, about an inch square and half an inch thick; cut out of some slices of good bacon some pieces an inch square also, but about a quarter the thickness of the mutton; cut up some pieces of parboiled white onion upon the same pattern as the bacon, and some thin slices of green ginger to match.

Impale these mixed pieces upon small plated or silver skewers, or upon thinly-cut wooden ones, maintaining the order I have given, *viz.*, first a piece of mutton, then a piece of bacon, then a bit of onion, and lastly, the thin slice of green ginger. Having repeated this until the skewer is filled, go on with another. When all have been completed, the *kubábs* should be simmered in a good curry sauce as recommended for chicken curry. Before being added to the sauce, however, they should be lightly tossed in butter in a *sauté*-pan with an onion sliced, a tea-spoonful of salt, and one of sugar. The introduction of the slice of bacon is a very great improvement.

The 'QUOORMA,' if well made, is undoubtedly an excellent curry. It used, I believe, to be one of the best at the Madras Club, in days when curries commanded closer attention than they do now.

Cut up about a pound of very tender mutton without any bone, and stir the pieces about in a big bowl with a dessert-spoonful of pounded green ginger, and a sprinkling of salt. Melt a quarter of a pound of butter in a stew-pan, and throw into it a couple of white onions cut into rings, and a couple of cloves of garlic finely minced. Fry for about five minutes, and then add a tea-spoonful of pounded coriander-seed, one of pounded black pepper, half one of pounded cardamoms, and half one of pounded cloves. Cook this for five minutes, then put in the meat, and stir over a moderate fire until the pieces seem tender, and have browned nicely. Now, take the pan from the fire, and work into it a strong infusion obtained from four ounces of well-pounded almonds, and a breakfast-cupful of cream. Mix thoroughly, adding a dessert-spoonful of turmeric powder, and a tea-spoonful of sugar. Put the pan over a very low fire, and let the curry simmer as gently as possible for a quarter of an hour, finishing off with the juice of a couple of limes. This, it will be perceived, is another curry of a rich yet mild description. The total absence of chilli, indeed, constitutes, in the opinion of many, its chief attraction.

According to the ancient canons by which the service of curries was regulated, CHUTNEYS of various kinds were considered as essentially necessary as the lordly platter of rice which, of course, accompanied them. These may be divided into two distinct classes: the preserved or bottled chutneys, and those that are made of fresh materials on the spot. Of the former I need say nothing: they are easily procured, and most people know the kind that suits them best. But concerning the latter, I think a little reflection will be found advantageous. There can be no doubt that the presentation of these chutneys, – the little *hors d'œuvres*, so to speak, of the curry service, – has of late years passed quietly into desuetude. This has been the result, to be sure, of the disappearance of curries from the *menu* of the modern dinner, and the very moderate degree of attention that they now command at our hands. Assuming, however, that those who still occasionally patronize the dish would rather see it at its best, and served correctly than not, I will go on with a few recipes that will be found easy enough.

Fresh chutneys should be served in saucers which should be tastefully arranged upon a tray. Four or five varieties can be presented together, so that there may be an opportunity of selection.

Caviare dressed with a few drops of lime juice and a dust of yellow pepper; roes of fish pounded with a little butter; potted prawns; potted ham; crab paste; lobster paste; and sardine paste, are *hors d'œuvres* that can accompany the chutneys and materially assist them.

The best fresh chutneys are: tomato, cucumber, mint, brinjal, cocoanut, mango or apple, tamarind, and potato.

For *tomato chutney:* – Remove the seeds and watery juice from two or three ripe tomatoes, chop them up with a quarter their bulk of white onion, and season the mince with a little salt; add a pinch of salt, two green chillies chopped small, and a little bit of celery also chopped, give the whole a dust of black pepper, and moisten it with a tea-spoonful of vinegar – anchovy vinegar for choice.

For *cucumber chutney:* – Cut the cucumber into thin strips an inch long; say three heaped up table-spoonfuls; mix with them a tea-spoonful of finely-minced onion, one of chopped green chilli, and one of parsley; moisten with a dessert-spoonful of vinegar in which a pinch of sugar has been dissolved, a dessert-spoonful of salad oil, and dust over it salt and black pepper at discretion.

Brinjal chutney is made in this manner: – Boil two or three brinjals, let them get cold, scrape out the whole of the inside of the pods, pass this through the sieve to get rid of the seeds. Rub a soup-plate with a clove of garlic, empty the brinjal pulp therein, dress it with a tea-spoonful of minced onion, one of green chilli, one of vinegar, and a very little green ginger, season with salt and black pepper, pat the mixture into a little mould, and serve in a saucer.

Cocoanut chutney consists of pounded cocoanut, flavoured with minced onion and green chilli, green ginger, and an atom of garlic, moistened with tamarind juice, and seasoned with red pepper and salt.

Mint chutney is made in the same way, substituting pounded mint for cocoanut. Scald the mint leaves before pounding them.

Mango or apple chutney is made like cucumber chutney with the addition of a tea-spoonful of chopped green ginger.

Tamarind chutney is a good one: – Pound together a table-spoonful of tamarind pulp and one of green ginger, season it with salt, a tea-spoonful of minced green chillies, and one of mustard seed roasted in butter; mix thoroughly and serve.

Mashed potato chutney is flavoured with minced onion, green chilli, salt, pepper, vinegar, and a pinch of sugar. With these relishes, curries are undoubtedly far nicer than when sent up unassisted.

Treacher's tinned *Bombay ducks* when presented with curries only require crisping in a brisk oven.

Papodums may either be toasted on a griddle over some clear embers, or fried in hot fat. Thin slices of raw brinjal, and green plantains, similarly fried, like potato chips, are nice with curries.

MULLIGATUNNY

If it be admitted that the knack of curry-making has gradually passed away from the native cook, I think it must also be allowed that a really well-made *mulligatunny* is, comparatively speaking, a thing of the past. Perhaps, then, a few words regarding this really excellent, and at times, most invigorating soup may be acceptable. In attempting this, I am anxious to address my observations to vegetarians, as well as to those who have no objection to eat meat, for I hope to be able to show that a very excellent *mulligatunny* can be made without any assistance from flesh or fowl.

This preparation, originally peculiar to Southern India, derives its name from two Tamil words – *molegoo* (pepper), and *tunnee* (water). In its simple form, as partaken of by the poorer natives of Madras, it is, as its name indicates, a 'pepper-water' or *soupe maigre*, which Mootoosamy makes as follows: – He pounds together a dessert-spoonful of tamarind, six red chillies, six cloves of garlic, a tea-spoonful of mustard seed, a salt-spoonful of fenugreek seed, twelve black peppercorns, a tea-spoonful of salt, and six leaves of *karay-pauk*. When worked to a paste, he adds a pint of water, and boils the mixture for a quarter of an hour. While this is going on, he cuts up two small onions, puts them into a chatty, and fries them in a dessert-spoonful of ghee till they begin to turn brown, when he strains the pepper-water into the chatty, and cooks the mixture for five minutes, after which it is ready. The pepper-water is, of course, eaten with a large quantity of boiled rice, and is a meal in itself. The English, taking their ideas from this simple composition, added other condiments, with chicken, mutton, &c., thickened the liquid with flour and butter, and by degrees succeeded in concocting a *soupe grasse* of a decidedly acceptable kind.

Oddly enough, we undoubtedly get the best *mulliga-tunny* now-a-days in England, where it is presented in the form of a clear, as well as in that of a thick, soup. In an artistic point of view, the former is infinitely the better of the two, as I shall endeavour to explain later on. Nevertheless, the thick is by no means to be despised. The superiority of the English adaptation needs but little explanation, for it may safely be attributed to the fact that the soup is composed upon a really strong foundation in the shape of stock, an important point that most Indian cooks slur over.

This reminds me of an anecdote, which an old friend and fellow-enthusiast on the subject of cookery, communicated to me as follows: – He was at home on furlough, and happened to visit an old uncle, whose early years had been spent in the Navy. The Admiral (for the old gentleman had attained that rank) was of a somewhat dictatorial nature, and had acquired a habit of asserting his opinions with a closed fist and vehement superlatives. Conversation one day turned upon *mulligatunny*, and the ancient mariner declared vociferously that he had never tasted the soup properly made since serving in the West Indies in the *Penelope* frigate in the year 1823, angrily shutting up his nephew for daring to observe that it could be fairly well prepared in the East. Now, my friend was far too wise in his generation to contradict his uncle, 'but,' said he, 'I determined to circumvent him.' Accordingly when, after some little time, the Admiral went up to London, he was lured into an ambuscade at his nephew's house. 'I made the *mulliga-tunny* myself,' said my friend, 'the basis of which was a good veal stock, prepared, of course, the previous day. My method of procedure was as follows: – I cut up a large sweet onion into fine rings, and fried them in two ounces of good butter, till about to turn yellow. I then stirred in three table-spoonfuls of Barrie's Madras *mulligatunny* paste, adding sufficient stock to bring the mixture to the consistency of *mayonnaise* sauce. This I tasted, and, finding that it required a little sub-acid, I administered a table-spoonful of red currant jelly and a few drops of lemon juice. Having stirred this in well, I put in a dessert-spoonful of Madras chutney, and added stock enough to produce a thin soup – about three pints in all. This I allowed to simmer (to extract the flavours of the various ingredients) for a quarter of an hour, while I pounded four ounces of sweet almonds in a mortar with a little milk, using a breakfast-cupful altogether. When fully pounded, I strained the almond milk into the soup, and stopped the simmering. The next step was to pass the whole of the liquid through a tin strainer into a clean bowl to catch up lumps of onion, chutney, &c. The *mulligatunny* having been skimmed, was now ready, all but the thickening. This process was carried out in due course, with two ounces of butter and two of flour. The soup was brought to boiling-point, and, off the fire, just before serving, a coffee-cupful of the best cream I could get was stirred into the tureen as the soup was poured into it.' When this was presented to the Admiral, the old gentleman was delighted, and, altogether forgetting his previous asseveration, exclaimed that he had not eaten such a basin of *mulligatunny* since serving on the East India station in the *Cockatrice* in the year 1834.

'I knew,' concluded by friend, 'that the dear old man was thinking of "calipash" and "calipee" when he pitched into me on the previous occasion, but I was not such an ass as to suggest that he had made a mistake.'

This *recipé* of my friend's may be taken as a very good guide for a *mulligatunny* made with pure meat stock extracted from veal, mutton, beef, or fowl, and ready-made paste. Yolks of eggs may supply the place of cream, and cocoanut milk may be substituted for the *lait d'amandes*. The addition of either almond or cocoanut milk is, however, a *sine quâ non*, if the object be to obtain a soft, creamy, well-flavoured, thick *mulligatunny*. The straining must also be carried out carefully, and the thickening as well.

Rice is served with *mulligatunny*, but it is, I think, a mistake to do so. We do not call for rice with hare soup, game soup, or mock-turtle; why, then, should we ruin our appetites by taking rice with so satisfying a *potage* as *mulligatunny*? The custom has been handed down to us by our forefathers, who, of course, ate rice with their *mulligatunny*, as did the natives from whom they learnt the dish.

The object in a *clear mulligatunny* is to present a bright, sparkling *consommé* of the colour of clear turtle, with a decided flavour of *mulligatunny*, and slightly peppery. Now, if you try to communicate the flavour with ready-made curry-powder or paste, in which there is a certain quantity of turmeric, you will experience considerable difficulty in getting your soup bright and clear. *Pounded* coriander seed, too, is oily, and would probably cause trouble. So the easiest method is to put a muslin bag, containing the flavouring ingredients, into the soup kettle with the vegetables, and to remove it as soon as the *consommé* is satisfactorily impregnated with the wished-for aroma. The pepperiness is best imparted with a few drops of tabasco as a finishing touch, or of chilli-vinegar if tabasco be unobtainable.

The following proportions will, I think, be found satisfactory as far as the flavouring is concerned: – Two ounces of coriander seed, one ounce of cummin seed, one ounce of fenugreek or *maythee*, half an ounce of mustard seed, two cloves of garlic, a dozen black peppercorns, and four or five leaves of *kurreaphool*, or *kodia neem* (*karay-pauk*). All put into a muslin bag, without pounding or bruising, boiled with the soup, and removed as soon as the flavour is satisfactory. These quantities are estimated for above three pints of clear *consommé*; but as tastes vary in the matter of condiments, they are obviously susceptible of alteration at discretion.

I would abstain from the use of all ordinary spices for fear of disturbing the flavour derived from the curry-stuff. The soup itself may be ordinary *consommé*, *consommé de volaille* or *blond de veau*. Clear ox-tail thus flavoured is well-known at the Army and Navy Club in London under the name of *queue de bœuf à l'Indienne*.

Fish consommé, i.e., a stock made from fish and vegetables, makes a capital basis for a thick *mulligatunny*; and a *bisque* or *purée* of shell-fish, flavoured with curry-paste, is a right royal *potage*.

Vegetarians can fall back upon a stock composed of vegetables, *consommé de légumes*. This, artfully flavoured with a good *mulligatunny* paste, thickened with flour and butter, and enriched with *lait d'amandes*, cocoanut milk, cream, or raw yolks of eggs, will be found to make a most excellent *soupe maigre*.

The stock should be composed as follows: – Weigh, when trimmed and cut up, one pound, each, of carrots and onions. Throw them into a stew-pan, with half a pound of butter (tinned butter will do well), a bunch of parsley, and a couple of ounces of celery. Fry until the vegetables begin to take colour, then moisten with two quarts of hot water. Boil and skim, then put into the pan half an ounce of salt, a quarter ounce of black pepper-corns, and a pint measure of shelled green peas. Simmer for three hours, skim off any oil that may rise from the butter, and strain the broth into a basin through a tamis.

Be careful in using turnips. Unless they are very young they are apt to be overstrongly flavoured in this country. Leeks are invaluable; if available I would put half a pound of them in with the carrots; a few sprigs of thyme or marjoram are also useful. A pint of French beans may be used instead of, or in addition to, the peas. This *consommé* is, with a dash of white wine, quite fit to serve alone. Maccaroni or vermicelli may be added to it as a garnish, and grated Parmesan may accompany it.

For ordinary *mulligatunny maigre*, however, plain *eau de cuisson* may be employed. This most useful liquid is too often thrown away by ignorant native cooks, or annexed by the wary ones for their own food. It is the water in which certain vegetables have been boiled. As a matter of economy, house-keepers should make a note of this. Suppose you want to make a *salade cuite*, i.e., a salad of cooked vegetables, the water in which the carrots, onions, leeks, peas, flageolets, French beans, and young turnips are boiled will provide you with an excellent stock for ordinary white sauce, or *mulligatunny*.

The ordinary chicken or mutton *mulligatunny*, made without assistance in the way of stock, may, with some little pains, be sent up in better style than our cooks, as a rule, are satisfied with. We do not want a thin yellow liquid with queer-looking leaves and bits of fried onion floating in it. We ask for a smooth, creamy *potage*, free from any lump or floating substance, and garnished with a few choice pieces of the chicken or mutton of which it was composed.

Cut up a well-nurtured chicken or young fowl as if for *fricassée*, soak the pieces in cold water for a quarter of an hour, then slice up a couple of good-sized onions, and put them, with two table-spoonfuls of butter, into a stew-pan on a good fire. Fry the chicken and onions together till slightly browned, then pick out the chicken, and stir into the butter a couple of table-spoonfuls of *mulligatunny* paste or curry-powder (Barrie's 'Madras,' if possible). Cook the paste or powder with the butter and onions for five minutes, and then stir in a couple of pints of warm water. Add the chicken; and if the pieces are not quite covered, put in water enough to do so. Let the contents come to the boil, then ease off the fire, and simmer for half an hour very gently. While this is going on, pound a couple of ounces of almonds in a mortar, with a coffee-cupful of milk, give it a pinch of sugar, and let the mixture stand till wanted. Now, having ascertained that the chicken is quite tender, stir in a dessert-spoonful of good chutney, a tea-spoonful of red currant jelly, and a tea-spoonful of lime-juice, and, after five minutes' simmering, strain off the whole of the liquid into a bowl. Pick out the nicest pieces of chicken for garnish, and put them aside. Now, skim the surface of the liquid, and, when quite clear of grease, proceed to thicken it, using a table-spoonful of butter and one of flour, and stirring in the soup slowly. All having been poured in, strain into the saucepan the almond milk, using a piece of muslin in order to catch up the bits of nut. Let the *mulligatunny* come to the boil, and serve.

The chief points to observe are: – First, the use of a really good paste or powder; next the simmering and addition of a pleasant sub-acid; then the straining, skimming, and thickening; and lastly, the introduction of the almond milk. Instead of almond milk, cocoanut milk (the infusion of the nut, I mean) may be used, and a table-spoonful of cream, or a couple of raw yolks of eggs, may be stirred into the tureen with the soup, by degrees, just before serving. The choice pieces of chicken should also be served in the *mulligatunny*.

For mutton *mulligatunny* follow this recipe, substituting a neck or breast of mutton for the chicken.

It will be seen from these observations that, while there is no difficulty whatever in making *mulligatunny* of a superior, as well as of an ordinary kind, it is a soup that demands no little care and attention. Whether it is worth the trouble or not is a question that can only be decided by practical experiment. I have no hesitation in recommending the trial.

Camp Cookery

Although no doubt there are many of my readers who have by long experience acquired the knack of making themselves thoroughly comfortable under canvas, and who, being fond of nice food, and *au fait* in culinary science, contrive to eat and drink in camp as luxuriously as in cantonment, there must be, I take it, a good many travellers, sportsmen, soldiers, and others whose duties demand several months of tent-life *per annum*, who would like to pick up a wrinkle or two in the matter of cookery under difficulties.

A friend of mine, who in addition to his passionate devotion to *la chasse*, possesses the keenest affection for his dinner, assured me, once upon a time, that *good bread* was the back-bone of happiness, – gustatory happiness, that is to say, – in the jungle. In cantonment even, this man despised the miserable travesty called bread furnished by the native baker. They say that he once *saw it being made*, never thought of it again without a shudder, and preferred a home-made roll for ever afterwards. He carried his roll with him, so to speak, into camp, and with the aid of a talented servant, was able to bake hot, clean, white bread daily, at a distance of many marches from an English dwelling place. He used Yeatman's baking powder, imported Australian or American flour, and a little salt. Butter and milk were added in the case of his fancy *petit pain*, and he occasionally mixed oatmeal with the flour for variety.

I often envied my friend's bread, yet never took the trouble to follow his example until comparatively lately. My conversion was brought about by Mr. Woolf of 119, New Bond Street, who introduced me to the 'Acmé cooking stove,' and gave me many a *séance* with regard to the use of Yeatman's baking powder for which his firm are the London Agents. The man who could remain unconvinced after one of Mr. Woolf's pleasant demonstrations, would be a stoic indeed. You are shown how to make a pound loaf, – 'cottage' pattern, in rolls, or in the tin. This is placed in the stove oven whilst you examine the numerous clever contrivances for the kitchen, – principally American inventions, – which form the *spécialités* of the establishment. In less than half an hour the loaf, baked to perfection, is placed upon the table.

Now here are two invaluable articles for the dweller in tents: – a composition, perfectly climate-proof, by which he can turn out an excellent loaf of light, clean bread; and the oven to bake it in.

The 'Acmé Stove' is cheap, portable, strong, and easily managed. It is fed by mineral oil, kerosine or parafine, and in addition to the oven, provides the cook with a capital kitchen range adapted for boiling, stewing, frying, and even grilling. The size I recommend, after upwards of two years' experience of its working, – more than a year of that time having been spent at Madras, – is fitted with double wicks four inches wide. One of these stoves with its ordinary appurtenances can be purchased for £2, s.15. For that sum you have a capital oven, with baking dishes and a griddle, a radiator, a kettle, and a frying-pan. Ordinary sauce-pans of a certain diameter can be used with it. A Warren's cooking pot, fitted to the stove, is furnished for £1-1, and a griller for five shillings and six-pence. When not wanted for cooking, it can be used for heating a room, for which purpose, you use the radiator, or ornamental chimney, previously mentioned. Thus adjusted, it is also very useful for airing damp linen, or drying wet clothes; you have merely to place a large cir-cular basket over it, and spread the things thereon, for the chimney is so contrived that the heat radiates lat-erally, and there is therefore no chance of burning, scorching, or smoking.

In camp, the first thing the Acmé would do for you would be to boil the water for your tea: if a raw Decem-ber, or January morning in the Deccan, or on the plateau of Mysore, you would not object to the operation being performed *inside* your tent, for the warmth would be very pleasant. It would then bake the bread for your breakfast, and warm up any *réchauffé* destined for that meal at the same time. During the day it would make the soup, and in the evening be available for work for din-ner. I do not say that you could do without a charcoal fire, but the stove would do a large portion of the day's cooking, and in a way vastly superior to any ordinary fire, either in camp or cantonment. In soup-making, for instance, and in stewing operations, you possess the power of producing the exact amount of heat you need by turning down the wicks at will. I have made a *pot-au-feu*, in a Warren's kettle placed upon my Acmé, the like of which I defy a native cook to produce with a common

41

cook-room fire, simply on account of this regulating power. A gallon flask of kerosine oil should be made to fit the stove box for short periods of camp life. If a man were settled in a standing camp, or out in his district for an indefinite period, he would, of course, require a keg of oil. I use my stove for some hours daily, and my month's expenditure does not exceed ten quart bottles.

Another of Mr. Woolf's valuable inventions, which I can strongly advise the traveller to obtain, is the 'Lang spirit lamp': the large one costs five shillings and six-pence, and is a never failing source of comfort on a journey. In camp it would be found a most useful append-age to the Acmé stove for light work, such as boiling milk for coffee, cooking eggs in all sorts of ways, heating sauces, frying bacon, &c. I use mine for *omelettes* almost every day in cantonment, for which work it is admirably adapted. With a 'Lang lamp' you can make a cup of tea or coffee in the train, by the side of the road, on arrival at a public bungalow, or under a tree whilst the lascars are pitching your tent: and by its aid, and that of a small frying-pan, you can devil a biscuit, fry a rasher, poach an egg, or cook a kidney, to accompany the tea or coffee. It is fed by methylated spirit, a gallon of which would last for at least two months.

Having thus directed your attention to two excellent appliances for the camp kitchen, I will return to the sub-ject of baking bread, for your servants can always contrive a field oven for you without difficulty, which, though infinitely inferior to that of the stove, will per-form the task required of it fairly enough. But in wet weather, the owner of an Acmé will, of course, laugh and grow fat, whilst his neighbour with only Ramasámy's fine weather make-shift to fall back upon, will beg for bread.

I have baked at home regularly now for over two years using, for ordinary bread, Yeatman's baking powder, American flour, salt, and water; for fancy rolls, the same with butter, and milk; and have discovered, after many experiments, that in this country, the proportions of baking powder to flour which are laid down in the paper of directions accompanying each tin, have to be increased. For eight ounces of flour, for instance, I find that I have to use two tea-spoonfuls of Yeatman.

I may say without hesitation that very few bread-makers hit off perfection at starting. I struggled through many disheartening attempts, before I turned out the thing I wanted. The common mistakes are overworking the dough, and using too much liquid. The mixing of dough with the proper quantity of fluid can only be acquired by practice, and all beginners knead too heavily through over zeal. Watch a professor. The fair-haired *artiste* who demonstrates bread-making at Mr. Woolf's, makes a pound loaf with three-quarters of a tea-cupful of water; her touch is as light as a feather, and the dough is made with wonderful swiftness. I have taught my servant to use two wooden spoons to work his dough with, the result is satisfactory as regards the lightness of the bread, and to those who dislike eating food mauled by native fingers, the system is especially attractive. If by any chance your dough has been made too sloppily, and from its putty-like consistency, you feel convinced it will be heavy, bake it in a tin.

The paraphernalia of the home-baker should be: – a large enamelled iron milk basin, two wooden spoons, a flour dredger, scales to weigh the flour, some patty-pans for rolls, some small tins for ditto, a baking-sheet, a half pound and pound loaf tin, and a cake tin: these various things are not expensive, they should be kept in the house (when in cantonment) away from the cook-room, as clean as possible, and be scrupulously reserved for their own purposes. Having provided yourself with this equipment, you should use Yeatman's baking powder, the best imported flour you can get, oatmeal occasionally, salt, and either good butter made at home, or that of any well-known brand preserved in tin. Here is a reliable receipt for four nice breakfast or dinner rolls: –

> eight ounces of flour,
> one dessert-spoonful of good butter,
> two tea-spoonfuls of Yeatman's powder,
> one salt-spoonful of salt,
> four table-spoonfuls of milk.

Rub the butter into the flour with one of the wooden spoons after having spread the latter in the enamelled pan, sprinkle the salt over it, and mix your dough as lightly as you can, using both wooden spoons, and shaking the milk into the flour by degrees. When nicely formed, add the baking powder (last thing of all mark), stir it well into the dough, divide it into four equal portions, pat them into shape with the spoons, and place them in four patty-pans well buttered: These must be put on the baking-sheet, and slipped into the oven, which should have been heated to receive them to such a degree that you can hardly bear your hand inside it. The time taken in baking depends upon the sort of oven you employ: as soon as the rolls brown very slightly, having risen into nice round forms, they are ready. This recipe may be altered to *five* ounces of flour, and three of oatmeal, for a change.

'*French Rolls*': – Half a pound of flour, a dessert-spoonful of butter, one small egg, two tea-spoonfuls of Yeatman's powder, a salt-spoonful of salt, and four table-spoonfuls of milk. Work the butter thoroughly into the flour. Beat the egg up briskly with the milk, and strain it into another cup, dust the salt over the flour, and gradually add the eggy-milk till the dough is formed; then mix the baking powder into it thoroughly; form the dough into two nice oblong rolls, place them on a sheet of well buttered paper, on the baking tin, and set them in the oven; look at them after twenty minutes' baking, and take them out as soon as their colour indicates that they are done.

'*Half pound plain loaf*': – Half a pound of flour, two tea-spoonfuls of Yeatman's powder, a salt-spoonful of salt, and four or five table-spoonfuls of water. Work this as above, reserving the baking powder to the last, set the dough in a tin, or form it in the well-known 'cottage' shape, and bake.

The ordinary cookery book receipts for fancy breads can be safely followed if you remember the proportion of the baking powder to the pound of flour, and, where eggs are propounded, make an allowance for the difference which exists between the English and the Indian egg. In using Yeatman's powder, do not let your *made* rolls, or bread, stand waiting for the oven: see that your baking apparatus is all but ready before you commence making the bread. You will observe that I recommend the baking powder to be put into the dough, *not* mixed with the flour in a dry state to start with. In London Mr. Woolf follows the latter method. I cannot explain what causes it, but I have found that the bread never turns out so satisfactorily *here*, if the powder be put in early: the temperature may have something to do with this; at all events, experience seems to show that the powder expends its effect to a great extent, during the working of the dough, if mixed with the flour first; whereas, if put in as a finishing touch, the bread being rapidly consigned to the oven, the result is invariably satisfactory.

I advise home-bakers to make *rolls* rather than large loaves. There is less waste with them. A roll is either eaten *in toto* or left untouched. If intact, you have merely to dip it in milk, and put it into the oven – damp; it will turn out again almost as freshly as a new roll. Bread, once cut, is apt to get dry, and with the exception of being sliced for toast, or grated for bread-crumbs, is not very presentable a second time. In baking, be very careful that your flour is well sifted and thoroughly dry. In a moist climate like this it is advisable to dry it in the oven before using it; the sifting must be carried out by a sieve. I have made very eatable bread with carefully sifted country flour, the sifting of which is an imperative necessity, be it observed, unless you have no objection to a gravelly loaf.

Now, let us discuss the animal and vegetable food of camp life, taking soups first: –

Many people think that because they cannot get beef in camp, they cannot have a freshly-made soup. Now, there are a few capital soups requiring no meat at all, which are known as '*soupes maigres*.' I will give you two: –

'*Soupe à l'oignon*': – Slice a couple of Bombay onions; powder them well with flour, let them fry awhile in a stew-pan with plenty of butter; before they begin to brown at all, add water, pepper, and salt, let the whole boil till the onions are well done and serve with *croûtons* of fried bread. Grated Parmesan should accompany.

'*Soupe aux choux*': – Let us assume that you have taken a cabbage or two with you when you left cantonment. Cut the cabbage into quarters, put them into a sauce-pan with a good sized slice of bacon, some slices of a Bologna sausage, and a bag containing sweet herbs, a clove of garlic, pepper, and a little spice; add water enough to cover the whole, and let the soup simmer till the cabbage is done, serve with *croûtons* of fried bread. A bacon bone would assist the undertaking greatly.

But you need not condemn yourself to '*soupes au maigre*' whenever there are sheep, and fowls, to be had, when you can shoot game, and lastly, when you are provided with tinned soups, and preserved vegetables, especially that excellent tablet called '*Julienne*.' In camp, bottles of dried herbs, and tinned provisions are, of course, indispensable, and you should be provided with potatoes, carrots, and onions before starting.

Soups in tins can be turned to excellent account in this way: – Kill a good full-sized fowl, cut it up, and put it, giblets and all, into a stew-pan; cover it with water, and let it come very slowly to the boil, skimming off the scum which may rise during that process; when the boiling stage has been attained, take the pan from the fire for a minute and throw into it a Bombay onion, cut into quarters, any fresh vegetables you may have brought out, a bag of mixed sweet herbs, a clove of garlic, a dozen pepper corns, a pinch of parsley seed, a few drops of celery essence, a table-spoonful of mushroom ketchup, a tea-spoonful of sugar, and a dessert-spoonful of salt. Now, let the pan boil again till the onion is soft, and then reduce the fire for the simmering stage. When the pieces of fowl are nice and tender, the broth is ready: long cooking will avail nothing: so lift up your pan, and strain off the broth into a bowl, it will be beautifully bright and clear; slightly tinted with *caramel* and served hot with a dessert-spoonful of Marsala and a dissolved dessert-spoonful of '*Julienne*,' this *consommé de volaille* will be found sufficient for two hungry men. When used in connection with a tin of soup, the broth should be poured from the bowl into the pan again, and the tin of soap added to it; a slow process of boiling should now be commenced, during which any scum the soup may throw up should be studiously removed, for all tinny impurities will thus be got rid of: when all but boiling, a table-spoonful of Marsala should be added, and the soup served. The pieces of fowl if not over-cooked, may be served in the form of fricassee, or be bread-crumbed or dipped in batter and fried, and served with maccaroni and tomato conserve.

Very valuable stock, remember, can be made from cold *roast* mutton bones – (do not try *raw* mutton, the taste will be tallowy) – assisted by bacon skin, bones and trimmings, a thick slice of Brunswick or Bologna sausage, and a chicken, or any game you can spare. Birds that have been mauled in shooting can thus be utilized. *Purées* of game can be made if you have taken out your utensils; if not, you must make the game broth as strong as possible, helped by a fowl as stock, and thicken it with flour. The addition of Marsala or port is, of course, a *sine quâ non*.

Tinned fish served, – as you sometimes see salmon at a dinner party, – plainly, and *hot* is positively nasty, and in no way improved by a *cold* sauce like tartare. Who, after a moment's reflection, could send up *hot* fish with a *cold* sauce? Preserved salmon, fresh herrings, and other tinned fresh fish, if served with *tartare* or *mayonnaise* sauces should be served *cold*, after having been carefully drained on a sieve from all the tinny juices which adhered to them. Select nicely sized pieces, place them on a dish with any garnish you may have such as *olives farcies*, capers, sliced gherkins, and rolled anchovies, and send the sauce round in a boat.

If you want a hot dish of tinned fish, you must choose the nicest pieces and gently warm them up in a rich *matelote* sauce, *velouté* or *poulette*, or you must wrap them in oiled paper and broil them a moment. All trimmings and odd bits can be saved and worked up as *rissoles*.

Fresh-water fish is often to be had by men out in camp. In cooking them, many recipes for filleted fish may be followed: clean them thoroughly, wash them well to get rid of all muddy taste, scale, trim, and soak them after cleaning, in water. A fish like *murrel* may be treated like a pike: – after having been carefully cleansed and trimmed, stuff it with turkey forcemeat sew it up, trim it in a circular shape with its tail in its mouth and bake it in a pie-dish surrounded by chicken stock about half an inch deep. A glass of any white wine like hock, chablis, or sauterne may be put into the stock, an onion also, and any vegetables you can spare. The fish should be basted every now and then, and when it has absorbed the gravy and seems soft, take it out of the oven. Put a pat of *maître d'hôtel* butter on the top of it, and serve in its own dish with a napkin folded round it. A good sized *murrel* will take from twenty minutes to half an hour in baking. A stuffing made with a tin of oysters, well drained and cut up, mixed with a half pint of bread-crumbs soaked in milk or stock, some spiced pepper, a little chopped very finely pared lime peel, and a couple of minced anchovies, all stirred together, and bound with a couple of eggs, is highly acceptable with a *murrel*. If you have no oysters, pound a good quantity of *fresh-water shrimps*, and mix them with the stuffing.

Eels ought to be slightly boiled first, whatever you do with them, you then get rid of their oiliness. After being thus treated, you can cut them into fillets for frying, for stewing, or for a pie. Eel fillets dipped in batter, and fried in oil or fat (lots of it) with a plain sharp sauce are delicious.

Tinned Australian, and other preserved lumps of meat, are valuable additions to the store box of the jungle-wallah, but they require very delicate handling, because they are almost always overdone. The really nutritious part of a tin of Australian meat is the gravy that surrounds it. Ramasámy knows this, so beware of unrighteous dealing, see the tin opened, and have every atom of the gravy strained off into a bowl. In cold weather, during such nights as you have in the Deccan during December and January for instance, the gravy in these tins becomes a jelly, so before you open one, set it on the fire in a sauce-pan surrounded by hot water for ten minutes or so; then open it, and strain the gravy from the tin into a bowl; turn the meat out carefully upon your sieve, and pour some hot water gently over it; catch the water in a bowl below the sieve, and add it to the gravy. Now, the gravy of a two-pound tin of beef will, as a rule, give you an excellent stock for two basins of soup: – skim the fat that may rise to its surface, and put it into a sauce-pan with a bag of dried sweet herbs, an onion cut into quarters, any vegetables you can spare, some pepper-corns, a pinch of spice, and salt according to the quantity: simmer this gently to extract the flavour of the things you have added, and in about a couple of hours you will have an excellent *consommé*, quite fit to be served as soup, with maccaroni, vermicelli, a couple of poached eggs, or Julienne, grated cheese accompanying; a table-spoonful of Marsala will be a grateful finishing stroke. Or it may be thickened like mock-turtle, and served with force-meat balls.

The meat should be treated in this way: – choose the nicest looking pieces, trim them neatly, and if of a fair size, brush them over with egg, bread-crumb them, and brown them in the oven, serving a good sauce, – tomato, *soubise*, or *piquante* for instance, with them. Or you can cut the meat into collops, and hash them very gently in a carefully made gravy. Lastly, you can mince it and serve it in many nice ways.

An excellent method may be thus described: – Having made your mince and flavoured it with a little chopped olive, anchovy, sausage meat, &c., bind it with a little good sauce thickened with a couple of eggs, and let it get cold: make a good sized thin pan-cake, take it from the pan when almost done, put it on a dish, and arrange some slices of cold cooked bacon upon it, lay the mince upon the bacon, give it a dust of spiced pepper, and fold the pan-cake over it: brush it over with an egg, bread-crumb it, and bake it a golden brown in your oven. The pan-cake should be just large enough to envelope the mince in *one fold* securely.

If you look upon a tin of preserved meat as a dish that has been cooked once, and has accordingly to be dressed *en réchauffé*, you will not fail to turn it to good account. But warmed up as it comes from the tin, unaided, and carelessly dished, it presents an irregular mass of sodden and tasteless diet which few would care to touch unless driven to do so by the calls of ungovernable hunger.

Messes like Messrs. Crosse and Blackwell's 'ducks and green peas,' 'Irish stew,' 'ox cheek and vegetables,' &c.,

should be avoided carefully, but if you find that your butler has sent such things to camp, you must pick the meat out of its surroundings, dress it with some fresh chicken meat, as a *rissole*, *croustade* or a mince, and cook the gravy and vegetables with some fresh chicken broth as a sauce.

I have already spoken of tinned vegetables, and also of the produce of the country. The traveller ought to try and find out what country garden stuff can be got from the villages near his camp. The recipes I have given will be found easy, and the monotony of tinned food will be much relieved by an occasional nicely dressed dish of common vegetables.

I will conclude this chapter with three very reliable recipes for cooking a hare. If you have shot the hare yourself so much the better, for then you will not find its heart, liver and kidneys gone. Skin, clean, and wash the animal well, saving the three parts I have mentioned carefully, *and the blood*. When quite clean, wipe the carcass inside and out, and let it soak in a *marinade* [see p. 54] all day, turning it every now and then. As the hour for cooking approaches, fill the hare with a well-made stuffing as for turkey. The kidneys and heart should be minced, and fried in fat bacon, with a little onion; when done, the contents of the pan should be poured into a bowl to cool, and when cold, pounded to a paste, and mixed with the stuffing. The back of the hare should be larded, or covered with thin slices of bacon pinned down with little skewers, it should then be roasted, a constant basting of melted butter or clarified beef suet being kept up throughout the process. When nearly done, the bacon strips should be removed, and the back lightly dredged with flour; the skin should be allowed to brown, and run into crisp blisters: the hare should then be served, – with a sauce made as follows: –

First make a good pint of the best gravy you can: cut the liver into dice, take a small sauce-pan, melt an ounce of butter in it, throw into it an onion finely shredded, toss the onion till it colours nicely, then throw in the chopped liver, shaking the pan for a minute or two: next add a little gravy, stir well, pour in all the gravy and simmer till the liver is cooked. Now, strain the gravy, pour into it the *marinade* of port wine, vinegar, ketchup, and red currant jelly in which the hare was soaked, put it on the fire in a sauce-pan, and pour in very slowly as it warms the *blood* you saved in the first instance; continue stirring, and the sauce will thicken, throw into it the liver pounded to a paste, stir and serve very hot.

Ramasámy sometimes envelopes his hare in a coating of light batter. Pray caution him never to do so again.

'Jugged hare' is perhaps the best dish for camp life; by many it is considered in *any* circumstances the best. This is a simple recipe: – Proceed as in the foregoing receipt as far as the skinning and cleaning is concerned. When ready, cut the hare up into neat pieces, dredge them with flour, and give them a few turns in the frying-pan with some butter till they take colour. Prepare beforehand a pint and a half of good strong stock (that of a fowl will do in camp) and choose a vessel that you can close securely with paste: put the pieces of hare into it, with two carrots, two or three large onions, an ounce of celery, the juice of two limes, a table-spoonful of sugar, and one of salt; pour in the stock, throw in *a wine-glass of brandy*, and seal the vessel as closely as possible; place it in a pan of cold water, and set it to boil, steaming the covered pot for three hours. When done, open the pot, stir into it a bumper glass of port, a dessert-spoonful of red currant jelly, and a lump of butter rolled in flour. Serve with a dozen balls of stuffing made as for roast hare, and fried in butter. Instead of steaming the jar, it may be placed in the oven and baked for two or three hours.

An excellent hash may be made of a cold roast hare in this way: – Trim off as much of the meat as you can find in slices, and cut out what remains of the stuffing: break up all the bones and put them with the skin and scraps into a stew-pan with a large onion cut up, pepper-corns, a bit of celery if possible, and any vegetable, a little spice, any sauce that may have been left, a couple of glasses of red wine and enough water to cover the bones, &c., simmer these ingredients for an hour and a half, and then strain off the gravy. Thicken it with butter and flour, flavour it with a dessert-spoonful of red currant jelly, a table-spoonful of mushroom ketchup, half a glass of vinegar, and a little more red wine: heat up the slices of hare in this sauce taking care that they do not boil, and serve with the stuffing sliced and fried in butter as a garnish.

I have found the process of 'jugging' very effective with venison, especially with jungle-sheep. The neck and breast can be utilized in this manner.

Many of the dishes detailed in the previous chapters will be found practicable in the camp; in short, if the pilgrim be blessed by the possession of an intelligent cook, and provided with a judicious assortment of culinary necessaries and stores, his tent life should never fail to possess amongst its many attractions that indubitably important one – a really good dinner.

On Coffee-Making

On certain occasions in the course of my jottings, I have mentioned the cup of *café noir* as the finishing touch of a nice little dinner. I think, therefore, that I may as well say a few words regarding its composition before I ask you to consider my *menus* ended.

Although few may think themselves ignorant of coffee-making, I question whether its real secrets are generally known. Indeed to judge by the stuff that we usually get, I think, we may say that the art is comparatively rare. First, to be sure, you must 'catch your coffee,' *i.e.*: – get really good berries, and be willing to pay a trifle over the usual price for them. That done, the next thing to learn is the roasting, an operation that should be conducted *daily* if you want well-flavoured coffee. The process is by no means as easy as many believe; half the coffee we drink is ruined by ignorant roasting; a burnt berry, mark you, will spoil the whole brew. The best way, I think, to roast the berries is to do a few at a time in a frying-pan over a *very low* fire, passing them straight to the mill (a *hand-mill* is quite indispensable) from the pan. A table-spoonful of berries will be found quite enough at a time. Melt a little butter, sufficient to lubricate the berries, and stir them about until they turn a light Havannah brown; if perchance a berry take a darker tint, throw it away as you would a reptile; grind them *at once* as coarsely as your mill will admit, – the grains should be quite as large as those of rifle gun-powder, – and make the coffee as soon afterwards as possible.

A little butter or salad oil is strongly recommended, it prevents the escape of much of the fragrance of the berry while roasting, and becomes quite dried up before the roasting is finished. The custom in the Indian kitchen is to bake, often to *over-bake*, the berries and then *tunny-cutch ammah* pounds them to a dull black powder as fine as flour. The result is a leaden tinted liquid, acrid in flavour, and repulsive to look upon.

Having ground the coffee properly, – it should be rich in aroma, and of a beautiful pale snuff colour – the best coffee-pot to use, after all, is the percolator. Be liberal with the coffee (a table-spoonful for each person), heat the coffee-pot thoroughly, fill the upper chamber of the percolator according to your requirements, ram the coffee down firmly, and having previously measured the amount of coffee liquid you require, pour boiling water, according to that measurement, *in tea-spoonfuls at a time*, through the upper strainer upon the powder. The slower the water is added, the more thoroughly the coffee will become soaked, and, the dripping being retarded, the essence will be as strong as possible. As soon as the coffee has run through, pour the rich essence you have obtained into your cups, and for *café au lait* fill them up with boiling milk, for *café noir* with a little boiling water.

As it is scarcely possible for your servant to make coffee with all this care at the end of a dinner party, I recommend that the essence be made just *before* dinner,

Notes from Madras

and kept covered up. For a party of twelve, two brews will be required. At the time it is wanted, the boiling milk imparts quite enough heat to the essence in the case of *café au lait*; and, for black coffee, a gentle re-heating, *plus* the modicum of boiling water aforesaid, insures a good cup; only, do not forget to pass round with it a flask of *cognac vieil*. I have confined my remarks to the method which I have followed for years success-fully, but there are, of course, other ways of making good coffee.

The Turkish system much praised by travellers may be thus described: – The roasting having been conducted with all the care I have already indicated, the berries are cast into a large metal mortar, and pounded to a very fine powder. This is carefully sifted through a fine sieve, all coarse particles being rejected. As much water as is wanted is then boiled in a small copper can, having a narrow top and broad bottom. When the water boils, powdered coffee is added, off the fire, according to requirements, and the can is replaced on the fire. The liquid is now permitted to come to the boil three times, the can after each occasion of ebullition being taken off the fire for a while. After the third boiling up, the can is placed for a minute in a shallow vessel containing cold water to precipitate the 'grounds,' after which the coffee clear, black, and sparkling is poured into the cup. For this I have to thank Colonel H. M.

Our Kitchens in India

Remembering as we all can so well the cheerful aspect of the English kitchen, its trimness, its comfort, and its cleanliness, how comes it to pass that in India we continue year after year to be fully aware that the chamber set apart for the preparation of our food is, in ninety-nine cases out of a hundred, the foulest in our premises – and are not ashamed? In the matter of utensils, and the general accessories of culinary work also, – knowing what things are considered essentially necessary even in the quietest establishment at home, – why are so many of us satisfied with an equipment regarding the miserable inadequacy of which it would be as well to keep silence? Why, in short, in the one country are we scrupulously careful that our food shall be clean, and in the other at all times willing, apparently, to eat dirt?

Over and over again have revolting facts been discovered in connection with the habits and customs of the cook-room. But instead of striking at the root of the evil, and taking vigorous action to inaugurate reform, we are absolutely callous enough not only to tolerate barbarisms, but even to speak of the most abominable practices as jests! Though cognizant, that is to say, of the ingenious nastiness of our cooks, we shrug our shoulders, close our eyes, and ask no questions, accepting with resignation a state of things which we consider to be as inevitable as it is disgusting.

But stop a moment: – *is it inevitable?* Let us consider that point. The *fons et origo mali*, it seems to me, are to be detected without difficulty. Think, first of all, of the distances which as a rule separate our kitchens from our houses, and the fact that the room is part and parcel of a block of godowns – not unfrequently within easy access of the stables. Setting aside other considerations for a moment, do we not at once perceive here two grave evils: – in the first place that proper supervision of the kitchen is almost out of the question; and, in the second, that promiscuous gatherings of outsiders, – the friends, relations, and *children* (a fruitful source of dirtiness) of our servants, – can take place in it undetected? Again: the room is generally constructed with as little ventilation and light as possible, its position with regard to the sun is never thought of, and arrangements for its proper drainage are rare. As there is no scullery, or place for washing up, &c., the ground in the immediate vicinity of the kitchen receives the foul liquid (as well as all refused matter) which is carelessly thrown out upon it. The consequence is that hard by many a cook-room in this Presidency, there is a noisome cesspool containing an inky looking fluid, the exhalations from which can scarcely improve the more delicate articles of food which are sent from the house for preparation.

Now follow me into the room. It is as black as Erebus. The pungent smoke from yonder wood fire, upon which some water for a bath is being boiled, penetrates every crevice. There is no chimney, you see, so the wall, up which the smoke is creeping towards an opening in the roof, is lined by an ancient coating of soot. Observe the mass of patriarchal looking cobwebs depending from the rafters, and the floor of mother-earth, greasy, black, and cruelly uneven in its surface.

Pull yourself together now, for we are about to examine the kitchen table. It is, to begin with, a piece of furniture which it would be gross flattery to call a dresser. It is small, and very rickety. In colour it is a remarkably warm burnt umber. The legs which support it are begrimed with dust which has become coagulated from time to time by grease, and smoked a rich sable. If you wished to do so, you could scrape off this filthy tegument with your pen-knife to the depth of the sixteenth of an inch. The top of the table is notched and scored all over with wounds inflicted by the chopper, the edges are all worn down, and there are tell-tale marks which prove that it is the custom of the *chef* and his assistants to mince parsley, herbs, onions, aye the meat itself of which those 'chicken cutlets' that he delights to give you are made, upon the oily, nut-brown board.

What are that stone slab and roller for, with traces of last night's spinach upon them? O! they are the pet *articles de cuisine* of *tunny-cutch ammah* to whose delicate fingers is entrusted the making of chutneys, and all preparations which are presented to you in the form of pulp. The boiled vegetable, or whatever it may be, is turned out upon the slab, and she rolls the pin backwards and forwards until the desired consistency is attained. How does she scrape the rolling pin, and the edges of the slab during this process, and how does she *dish it*? Hush, my friend, *there is not a spoon in the kitchen.*

Cast your eye over that meagre array of degchees and of sauce-pans nearly as black inside as they are outside, and note that there is a spit there, a chatty oven in yonder corner, and – nothing more. There is no cupboard, neither is there a rack for plates and dishes, but such small *etcetera* as the cook uses are thrust at hap-hazard upon that shelf, which, in griminess, you see, matches the table, whilst it comes in handily for his turband, and the folded leaf containing his snuff. You have seen enough now, and look as if you wanted a brandy and soda, so let us return to the house.

On our way you inveigh against native filthiness, &c., &c. Come now, be just in your condemnations, for verily this is a case in which it behoves us to remember the beam which is in our own eye, before we seek diligently to pull out the mote which is in our black brother's eye. Who is really to blame for a great deal that I have shown you? Is it the cook's fault that a wretchedly mean, carelessly constructed godown is given him for a kitchen; that the place is inconveniently far from the house, and consequently open to every passer-by; that the furniture is absolutely nothing more than one table, far too small for culinary requirements, and one shelf; that owing to faulty construction, the room 'smokes' dreadfully, and that there is scarcely sufficient light in it to detect dirt? Is it the cook's fault that in the absence of proper appliances he is forced to practise his native ingenuity, to use chatties for sauce-pans and stew-pans, to use the 'curry-stone' for a mortar, his cloth for a sieve, and his fingers for a spoon or fork? Is it the cook's fault that, since no plates and dishes are included in his cook-room equipment, he has no alternative but to place meat, vegetables, &c., on his table; and that being without a mincing machine, or chopping board, he uses its surface in lieu of the latter? Why instead of denouncing the unfortunate man, I make bold to say that handicapped as he is, we have positively no reason to expect him to be clean!

Now I do not mean to say that the state of things that I have endeavoured to sketch obtains in every Madras establishment. On the contrary, I am quite sure that in some cases the utmost trouble is taken to make everything as clean and as nice as possible, that every available appliance is given to the cook with a generous hand, and that the mistress of the house prides herself upon visiting her kitchen and *seeing* that her orders are carried out. No: it is not to the energetic few that I dedicate these comments, but to the apathetic many who actually know not what they do – to themselves and to their friends – by permitting the preparation of their food to take care of itself. People who refrain from all interference, who hand everything over to their butlers, and take cleanliness for granted, do so, I know, sometimes through sheer ignorance, sometimes on account of idleness, and sometimes because they are not physically equal to the exertion. I frankly admit that the labour is frequently very disheartening. It strikes me, however, that if reform were made easier and pleasanter, many who are now content to let things 'slide' might wake up and become enthusiastic, while even those, who do not know what trouble means in the matter of perfecting their *cuisine*, would be thankful to find their daily task less irksome. Let us, therefore, briefly consider how that object might be achieved.

Taking the kitchen itself first: why on earth should we continue to accept as places fit for the cooking of our food the dismal hovels that are attached to our godowns, and called cook-rooms? These places may have sufficed for the culinary necessities of our forefathers, who chiefly preyed upon curry and rice, and lived to all intents and purposes *à la mode Indienne*. But *nous avons changé tout cela*. The delicate cookery which day by day gains popularity in India now demands a clean airy room, properly furnished, with plenty of *light*, and many accessories borrowed from civilized Europe.

It has become essential, in fact, that to every house there should be attached a small building reserved solely for kitchen work and – nothing else. It should be quite close to the house, and connected with the back verandah by a covered way. It should be constructed with a frontage towards the north or south so that the rays of the morning and evening sun may strike its sides. It should contain three rooms: – the work-room, the cooking-room, and the scullery, all opening into a good verandah.

In the first, the food, pastry, &c., should be prepared; it should therefore be well ventilated, and have a good glass window or sky light, a large dresser, a marble pastry slab, a rack for plates and dishes, shelves for cups, jugs, bowls, &c., a cupboard for culinary stores, and a gauze meatsafe to protect meat, &c., from flies. Communication between this room and the cooking-room should be shut off so that no smoke could find its way into it: things should be carried to the kitchen *viâ* the verandah.

The cooking-room should, if possible, contain an English or American range. Failing that, a country-made range upon English principles, the construction of which I will discuss by-and-by. It should be well ventilated, well lighted, and, in any circumstances, should contain a chimney. A table for dishing up, &c., would be required here, and also racks for ladles, dredgers, &c., with shelves for the utensils.

The scullery being merely used for washing up, the drawing, cleaning, and plucking of poultry, and work of that nature, would require a well made water-tight sink, communicating with an equally carefully made cistern, covered by a trap-door, outside the building: the cistern should be emptied every day, and well sprinkled with McDougall's disinfecting powder. A tap of Red Hills water in the scullery would be a great boon at Madras.

The floor of room number one might be of chunam matted over, that of number two should be paved with slabs of stone, and a similar one of stone should be laid down in the scullery.

The day's work having been completed, the doors of the three rooms should be carefully locked, and the whole *corps de cuisine* dismissed, the keys being brought to the mistress of the house. The idea of the kitchen being used by a number of native employés as a sleeping chamber is obviously too horrible to need more than a passing remark.

The two chief objections that will here suggest

themselves will be, I feel sure, on the one hand the difficulty of establishing the kind of kitchen I have described,
and, on the other, the expense of equipping it according
to the standard which obtains in England: I propose,
therefore, to deal with those points independently, taking
the kitchen first.

The little building that I advocate, – entirely separated
from the godowns, planned specially to meet culinary
requirements, close to the house, and connected with it
by a covered way, – in spite of its niceness theoretically,
is, I admit, practically speaking almost an impossibility.
Few owners of houses would go to the expense of a new
building. I nevertheless offer the idea to those who are
about to build *de novo*, and to such of my fellow country-
men, who, interested in houses that they have purchased,
may be tempted to make their 'offices' as complete, and
as home-like as possible.

In what way, then, can anything be done to improve
upon matters as they at present stand? Well, a great deal,
of course, depends upon circumstances. There are a
good many houses that possess small buildings close to
the back verandahs, which, I presume, were originally
intended to be used as a 'coolers' godowns,' or, perhaps,
for the hanging of meat. They cannot be of much use for
either of those purposes now-a-days, for the ancient
cooler's 'occupation's gone,' and the modern zinc-lined
safe has made as independent of a larder. It seems to
me, then, that some of these little places might be easily
converted into kitchens, large enough at all events to
accommodate one of the small yet very excellent Anglo-
American cooking ranges now procurable, together with

its accessories, and such things as are necessary for mere *cooking*. A place for washing up might easily be contrived on one side, or at the back of this room, and a light covered way might be thrown up cheaply enough to connect it with the house.

Assuming such an arrangement feasible, the sacrifice of some small back room on the ground floor of the house, or the walling off of a portion of the back ver-andah would still be necessary to provide the 'working room,' – the room, that is to say, in which all food should be *prepared* prior to being conveyed to the kitchen. This I may call one of the chief points of the system I advocate, for, I maintain, that for numerous undeniable reasons, the making of pastry, the dressing of meat and vegetables, and the mixing of sauces, puddings, &c., should be per-formed in a cool place, away from the smoke and heat of fires, where wind and dust can be excluded by closing the door, and yet ample light be obtained from a good glass window, and, above all things, where the *chef* can be easily supervised.

To illustrate the necessity of this recommendation, let us imagine that a cook, accommodated as he is at pres-ent, is engaged in preparing a *soufflé*, or some equally delicate *entremets*. Of a sudden a blast of wind drives a cloud of dust into the cook-room through the door (which is of necessity open to admit light), and blows myriads of fine particles of charcoal ashes from the open fire-places over everything. By-and-by the dish is served at dinner. *Monsieur le mari* cheerfully receives his por-tion, but presently encounters grit, and orders his plate to be taken away, murmuring something about the impolicy of petty economy in connection with flour. *Madame la châtelaine*, conscious of procuring the best of everything, replies – more in sorrow than in anger, yet withal warmly – and denies the unkind impeachment, though constrained to send her plate away also. And thus a cloud comes over what ought to be a very happy *tête-à-tête*, while indigestion, the natural result of irritation at meals, most probably follows.

Now the worst of it is that unless people happen to discover the real causes of accidents such as these themselves, they may wait until doomsday for enlightenment. The mental equilibrium of the native cook is in no wise disturbed by a dust storm, for he is perfectly accustomed to them; and the butler will assuredly invent a plausible excuse for the contretemps: – 'little bit yegg-shell,' or 'sugar mistake.' It therefore comes to this, that we must insist upon a nicer appreciation of the cleanliness and care that the preparation of food demands, and to accomplish that end satisfactorily a room of the kind I have described appears to me to be essentially necessary.

I am perfectly aware that, in some instances, every species of obstruction will at first be thrust in the way of those who try to follow my advice, and, in others, that the change will be obeyed with reluctance. But determination and tact combined will, I think, overcome opposition after a time, and the very malcontents themselves will end by praising the new *régime*.

It is downright nonsense to say that native cooks *cannot* work upon English principles. They manage very well on board ship, where their services are highly prized, yet their appliances are wholly European. The kitchen at the Madras Club, and those of several private houses, both here, and on the Hills, are fitted up entirely upon the Home system, yet the cooks do not complain. No: it seems pretty clear that if no other alternative present itself, Ramasámy can fall into the way of using a range readily enough.

I know of a case in which a young and zealous native *chef* absolutely begged his mistress to permit him to prepare his jellies, pastry, &c., in a spare room in the house, alleging as his reason that the kitchen was too hot and smoky: and I am perfectly sure that the majority of good Madras cooks would appreciate a similar concession. The recusants would, in all probability, be gentlemen who have become wedded to practices whereof their consciences are afraid. Pilferings of all kinds would, to begin with, become far more difficult, long absences would be soon detected, work properly the cook's could not be thrust upon the cook's maty, and drinking and gossiping during working hours would be knocked on the head.

The furnishing of this 'working room' could be managed without much trouble, and certainly inexpensively, in the manner already mentioned: – with a dresser of strong wood, a pastry table with marble slab, a cupboard, a rack for plates and dishes, a gauze safe, and a set of shelves. Delicate operations, such as the composition of high class sauces, the boiling of a jelly, or the simmering of fruit, could be carried on upon a mineral oil stove, or by means of a charcoal fire placed in a sheltered corner of the verandah close to the room; and such articles of diet need never be carried into the kitchen at all. But when properly dressed, and prepared for roasting, stewing, boiling, baking, &c., savoury meats, pastry, and puddings, would, of course, be transported to the cooking-room.

In cases where there is no isolated building near the house susceptible of conversion into a kitchen, the cook-room, such as it may be, would have to be utilized; but if properly ventilated, fitted up with a range, racks, tables, &c., frequently inspected, and reserved exclusively for the work I have mentioned, its evils might surely to be reduced to a minimum.

Another great thing to obtain, to my mind, is a really clean place, not only for the preparation of food, but also for its *keeping* during the day. Think for a moment of the dish of neck of mutton cutlets that the cook takes away to the cook-room at 10 A.M., after his mistress has inspected the market supplies. The cutlets re-appear at dinner time, it is true, but dare we consider how the poor things spent their day before the hour of their cooking arrived? In my ideal room they would be trimmed immediately upon a clean dresser, flattened with the cutlet bat, and then arranged neatly upon a large flat dish, dusted over with pepper and salt, lightly dredged with flour, and consigned till wanted in the gauze safe; or, if so required, they might be placed in *marinade*, and then put away beyond the reach of flies. The trimmings would, of course, be collected upon a plate, and sent out to the kitchen for the production of broth for sauce.

And now for a few words about kitchen ranges and equipments. Until almost the other day, so to speak, an

English range was regarded as too expensive a luxury for people in India of ordinary means. The expenditure of from two to three hundred rupees upon such a thing was looked upon as an extravagant freak. This strange opinion must have been born and bred in Hindustan a generation or more ago, and handed down to us together with numerous other baseless nostrums in the usual course of things; for people could scarcely have forgotten – even forty years ago – that dwellings built for persons of three hundred a year at home were considered uninhabitable unless equipped with a kitchen range that at least cost thirty pounds.

Of course, there was an excuse for the economy, one indeed, that is readily pleaded, I dare say, to-day: – An English range would be thrown away upon a native cook, he could never appreciate its advantages, and would fall back upon his own way of doing things the moment he was left to himself. With this ingenious subterfuge numbers of people have been contented, and have willingly closed their eyes year after year to the wastefulness, and barbarity, of the native system.

The consequence is that we now find ourselves in a somewhat anomalous position. Whereas our tastes have undergone a complete change for the better; whereas men of moderate means have become hypercritical in the matter of their food, and demand a class of cooking which was not even attempted in the houses of the richest twenty years ago, – our kitchens have been in no way improved, neither have their appliances or equipments undergone the change that is necessary to keep pace with the requirements of the times. Dinners of sixteen or twenty, thoughtfully composed, are *de rigueur*; our tables are prettily decorated; and our *menu* cards discourse of dainty fare in its native French. But what 'nerves' we all have to be sure! Could we but raise the curtain, and examine our cook-rooms, and all that in them is, just before we lead the way to the banquet, should we not be actually dumb-foundered at our own audacity?

Setting aside the things which I have already enlarged upon, it is no exaggeration to say that not one Indian kitchen in twenty possesses a proper equipment. The *batterie de cuisine* of people with incomes of two thousand rupees a month, and more, is frequently inferior to that of a 'humble cottager in Britain,' the total of whose means does not exceed four hundred pounds. But while the latter lives with consummate modesty, and thinks his establishment by no means equal to the strain of a dinner party of six, the former sits down, invites five-and-twenty people with a light heart, and expects everything to be of the best!

The nakedness of the land is easily discovered at the auctions of our highest officials, where the contrast between the 'furniture principally by Deschamps' in the drawing-room, and the 'few useful kitchen sundries' in the back verandah, is often very striking.

The loan system is also eloquent of the inefficient equipments of our neighbours. To meet the culinary wants of a dinner party at the Robsons', the Dobsons' ice-pail, fish-kettle, and sieves, are requisitioned; and *vice versâ*, when the Dobsons invite their friends, the

Robsons' kitchen is pillaged to the extent of a border mould, a ham boiler, and the pastry cutters.

Having, I hope, satisfactorily demonstrated that a kitchen range should surely find a place in the category of things to be 'devoutly wished for' by all who take any interest in their *cuisine*, let me now point out a few of the advantages to be derived from the use of one.

After having once set up a good range, the purchaser ought, in the first place, to experience a marked diminution in his fuel account. The native cook's objection 'too much firewood taking' is, let me observe, a downright perversion of fact. If properly understood, and utilized to its full extent, the English range, with its one fire, must surely consume less fuel than do the numerous open fires in an Indian cook-room. This is self-evident. According to the method that is followed in the latter system, a separate fire is required for each thing: – for the bath water, the kettle, the oven, the sauce and stew-pans, &c., &c. A range provided with a hot-plate, an oven, and a boiler, supplies with its one fire all these wants at once. Vessels, the contents of which require rapid boiling, are placed over the fire-hole, while things needing slow treatment, like soups, stews, &c., find a place upon the hot-plate, or flat surface of the range. The oven is, of course, always kept hot, and the boiler, if correctly filled, must contain an unceasing supply of hot water. If however these opportunities of economy be neglected, and if the cook be permitted to make up little fires, in addition to that of the range, here and there in the kitchen in his native fashion, the saving in fuel will, I grant, be small.

I know that the 'Duff's cooking ranges,' which are set up for the use of British soldiers in the barracks of this Presidency, are generally condemned by the men as requiring too much wood. But then they are not utilized in a way by which economy is attainable. T. Atkins requires no soup; he is not particular regarding the tenderness of the stew he eats; and he rarely wants hot water. He finds the oven alone necessary, for 'Jack,' the barrack cook-boy, can use the chatty, the grid-iron, or the frying-pan, in the verandah, over a small charcoal fire, with sufficient cleverness to satisfy his many masters. Yet the ranges in the hospital kitchens are thoroughly appreciated. Hot water is in constant requisition there, soup must be made daily, and meat has to be very carefully cooked. In order, then, to find English ranges economical as fuel consumers, people who buy them must take care that they are turned to their proper and full account.

The superior quality of the food cooked with a perfect appliance of this kind when compared with the best results obtainable by the native system, is another strong recommendation in favour of the range. Take one item of daily consumption – our soup. It is not exaggeration to say that, as a general rule, the native cook takes nearly double the amount of meat and bone necessary to produce this article of food. His doing so may be attributed, of course, in a great measure to ignorance; but he can also plead as an excuse the want of a proper kitchen equipment.

The extraction of the nutritive elements of meat and bone requires, we all know, that slow process of cookery called simmering – a process as readily carried out with an English range, as it is almost impossible with the open brick and mud fire-places of the cook-room. At least, it stands to reason that – be the *tunny-cutch* never so careful – the low fire, at an even degree of temperature, which simmering requires, can scarcely be maintained for hours together by the eye and hand alone.

With a range in our kitchen, therefore, all we should have to do would be to explain the simmering system, and point out how easily it can be managed. Then, as soon as the native cook discovered that all that was necessary was to pull his soup kettle so many inches back upon the hot-plate, he would do so, for the new plan would not interfere with his customary absence for 'rice.' In the end we should get a soup of superior quality extracted from about half the quantity of meat that we formerly issued.

In like manner all dishes requiring slow cookery, hashes, stews, sauces, – even our curries, which are often sent up tough from being too quickly cooked, – would be easily prepared, and certainly be far more digestible. The cleanliness of the system need not be dwelt upon, smoke would become a thing unknown, and ashes could no longer be wafted by every breeze into our food.

With so much to be said in favour of the kitchen range, it seems strange that its *cost* should be considered prohibitive by so many well-to-do people in India. If properly used the economies it effects must, in the end, repay its purchase, while it ought to be at all times a very saleable article. Why, I repeat, should we hesitate to provide ourselves in India with an appliance that in England is regarded by people of ordinary respectability as a common necessary of life?

Ingenious and painstaking persons who hesitate to go to the expense of an English range may, as I said before, effect a material improvement in their kitchen system by putting together a fire-place upon home principles. I know of a case in which an experiment of this kind has been crowned with success. The method followed may be briefly described as follows: –

A fire grate was first contrived by iron bars in the style of a cresset, rectangular in shape, and supported on four iron props; it was made the full length and height of an English kitchen grate, but one-third less deep at back. Embedded in masonry on one side of this fire grate was an iron bazár-made boiler; the side of it nearest the fire had no masonry, and it fitted closely to the iron bars. The boiler was furnished with a brass tap. On the other side of the grate, set firmly in masonry, with its side towards the fire exposed, and with a close fitting door was a bazár-made iron oven. The props of the cresset fire-place were set in masonry and cemented; they were sufficiently long to sustain the fire about the average height from the ground that kitchen fires are fitted in England. Over the top of the fire a flat sheet of iron connected the surface of the oven with that of the boiler, forming a very fair hot-plate. This iron sheet was movable at pleasure. The topmost outer bar of the cresset was also movable to allow a space for the admission of fuel when the hot-plate was fixed. The smoke was made to pass into a flue contrived with a few feet of ready-made stove piping, which passed through the wall of the kitchen at the back of the fire grate, and was then led up the wall to the roof.

But by far the best thing introduced in this locally designed kitchen was an English roasting 'jack.' The 'jack' itself was imported from home at a cost of half a sovereign; the fire screen and dripping pan were made by the bazár tinman; the 'jack' was hung from a beam fixed in the wall at a convenient height above the fire grate. Every joint was in this manner roasted *more Anglico.* Dripping, a thing previously unknown in the establishment, became a highly valued commodity; and the meat was invariably sent up full of gravy, and with that crisp browning that can only be obtained by carefully roasting. A little more charcoal was used in the 'jack' system than in the old way with the spit, but the expense was more than balanced by the dripping gained, the good gravy, and the additional juiciness of the meat. Charcoal was used for roasting work, and good dry wood was found sufficient for soups, and all common boiling operations, when no roasting was needed. The strange thing was that both the butler and the cook were as delighted with the innovation as children with a new toy. I hope that this may encourage some of my readers to carry out a similar scheme.

Finally: with a range (if possible), and with an arrangement, such as I have tried to describe, giving us a clean, nicely equipped room for the preparation of our food, and a kitchen, entirely separated from godowns and stabling, easily accessible from the house, and consequently continually subject to scrutiny and wholesome discipline, I think that the back-bone of the evils I have spoken of would be broken, ladies would find the supervision of their domestic economy a pleasure rather than a penance, and we should be able to congratulate ourselves upon having really laid the foundation-stone of true reform at last.

GREAT FOOD

RECIPES FROM THE WHITE HART INN

William Verrall

WILLIAM VERRALL, the redoubtable eighteenth-century landlord of the White Hart Inn in Lewes, Sussex, trained under a continental chef and was determined to introduce the 'modern and best French cookery' to his customers. Gently mocking Englishmen who eat plain mutton chops or only possess one frying-pan, he gives enthusiastic advice on must-have kitchen gadgets and describes enticing dishes such as truffles in French wine and mackerel with fennel.

This selection also includes the recipes that the poet Thomas Gray scribbled in his own well-thumbed copy of Verrall's *Complete System of Cookery*, which was one of the best-loved food books of its time.

'Racily written'
ALAN DAVIDSON

GREAT FOOD

THE CHEF AT WAR

Alexis Soyer

THE FLAMBOYANT FRENCHMAN Alexis Soyer was the most renowned chef in Victorian England. This is his colourful account of his time at the front in the Crimean War, where he joined British troops in order to improve the quality of the food they were eating.

Divulging the secrets of preparing stew for 1000 soldiers, sharing sweetmeats with a Turkish Pacha, and teaching a Highland regiment to cook with his pioneering gas-fuelled 'field stove' that would be used by armies up until the Second World War, Soyer gives a vividly enjoyable lesson in making a little go a long way.

'The first celebrity chef –
a kind of Anglo/French Jamie Oliver'
PETER MAY

BUFFALO CAKE AND INDIAN PUDDING

Dr A. W. Chase

TRAVELLING PHYSICIAN, SALESMAN, author and self-made man, Dr Chase dispensed remedies all over America during the late nineteenth century, collecting recipes and domestic tips from the people he met along the way. His self-published books became celebrated US bestsellers and were the household bibles of their day.

Containing recipes for American-style treats, such as Boston cream cakes, Kentucky corn dodgers and pumpkin pie, as well as genial advice on baking bread and testing whether a cake is cooked, this is a treasure trove of culinary wisdom from the homesteads of a still rural, pioneering United States.

GREAT FOOD

A DISSERTATION UPON ROAST PIG & OTHER ESSAYS
Charles Lamb

A RAPTUROUS APPRECIATION of pork
crackling, a touching description of hungry London
chimney sweeps, a discussion of the strange pleasure
of eating pineapple and a meditation on the delights
of Christmas feasting are just some of the subjects
of these personal, playful writings from early
nineteenth-century essayist Charles Lamb.

Exploring the joys of food and also our
complicated social relationship with it, these
essays are by turns sensuous, mischievous, lyrical
and self-mocking. Filled with a sense of hunger,
they are some of the most fascinating and
nuanced works ever written about eating,
drinking and appetite.

*'The Georgian essayist, tender and puckish,
with a weakness for oddity and alcohol,
is one of the great chroniclers of London'*
OBSERVER

··· GREAT FOOD ···

THE JOYS OF EXCESS

Samuel Pepys

AS WELL AS BEING THE MOST celebrated
diarist of all time, Samuel Pepys was also a hearty
drinker, eater and connoisseur of epicurean
delights, who indulged in every pleasure
seventeenth-century London had to offer.

Whether he is feasting on barrels of oysters,
braces of carps, larks' tongues and copious amounts
of wine, merrymaking in taverns until the early
hours, attending formal dinners with lords and ladies
or entertaining guests at home with his young wife,
these irresistible selections from Pepys's diaries
provide a frank, high-spirited and vivid picture
of the joys of over-indulgence – and the
side-effects afterwards.

*'Vigorous, precise, enchanting . . . the most ordinary and
the most extraordinary writer you will ever meet'*
CLAIRE TOMALIN

GREAT FOOD

THE ELEGANT ECONOMIST
Eliza Acton

BEFORE MRS BEETON THERE WAS Eliza Acton, whose crisp, clear, simple style and foolproof instructions established the format for modern cookery writing, leading to her being called 'the best writer of recipes in the English language' by Delia Smith.

Including such English classics as suet pudding, raspberry jam, lemonade and 'superlative mincemeat' as well as evocatively named creations like 'Threadneedle Street biscuits', 'Baron Liebig's beef gravy' and 'apple hedgehog', these recipes advocate using the best produce available to create wholesome, inexpensive dishes that are still a pleasure to cook and eat today.

'The best writer of recipes in the English language'
DELIA SMITH

GREAT FOOD

FROM ABSINTHE TO ZEST
An Alphabet for Food Lovers

Alexandre Dumas

AS WELL AS BEING THE AUTHOR OF *The Three Musketeers*, Alexandre Dumas was also an enthusiastic gourmand and expert cook. His *Grand Dictionnaire de Cuisine*, published in 1873, is an encyclopaedic collection of ingredients, recipes and anecdotes, from Absinthe to Zest via cake, frogs' legs, oysters, roquefort and vanilla.

Included here are recipes for bamboo pickle and strawberry omelette, advice on cooking all manner of beast from bear to kangaroo – as well as delightful digressions into how a fig started a war and whether truffles really increase ardour – brought together in a witty and gloriously eccentric culinary compendium.

'From the great French novelist and obsessive gourmet. The cook book as literature'
NORMAN SPINRAD

····· GREAT   FOOD ·····

EATING WITH THE PILGRIMS & OTHER PIECES

Calvin Trillin

ACCLAIMED *NEW YORKER* JOURNALIST, novelist and poet, Calvin Trillin is also America's funniest and best-loved writer about food. This selection of some of his wittiest articles sees him stalking a peripatetic Chinese chef, campaigning to have the national Thanksgiving dish changed to spaghetti carbonara and sampling the legendary Louisiana boudin sausage – to be consumed preferably 'while leaning against a pickup'.

Eschewing fancy restaurants in favour of street food and neighbourhood joints, Trillin's writing is a hymn of praise to the Buffalo chicken wing, the deep-fried wonton, the New York bagel and the brilliant, inimitable melting-pot that is US cuisine.

'Marvelously funny and horrifyingly mouth-watering'
ROLLING STONE

GREAT FOOD

THE PLEASURES OF THE TABLE
Jean-Anthelme Brillat-Savarin

EPICURE AND GOURMAND Brillat-Savarin was one
of the most influential food writers of all time. His 1825
book *The Physiology of Taste* defined our notions of French
gastronomy, and his insistence that food be a civilizing
pleasure for all has inspired the slow food movement
and guided chefs worldwide.

From discourses on the erotic properties of truffles
and the origins of chocolate, to a defence of gourmandism
and why 'a dessert without cheese is like a pretty woman
with only one eye', the delightful writings in this selection
are a hymn to the art of eating well.

*'Marvellously tart and smart, and also
comfortingly, absurdly French'*
AA GILL

GREAT  FOOD

THROUGHOUT the history of civilization, food has been livelihood, status symbol, entertainment – and passion. The twenty fine food writers here, reflecting on different cuisines from across the centuries and around the globe, have influenced each other and continue to influence us today, opening the door to the wonders of every kitchen.

THE WELL-KEPT KITCHEN..Gervase Markham

THE JOYS OF EXCESS ....Samuel Pepys

EVERLASTING SYLLABUB AND THE ART OF CARVING ....Hannah Glasse

RECIPES FROM THE WHITE HART INN ....William Verrall

A DISSERTATION UPON ROAST PIG & Other Essays ....Charles Lamb

THE PLEASURES OF THE TABLE ....Brillat-Savarin

THE ELEGANT ECONOMIST ....Eliza Acton

THE CHEF AT WAR ....Alexis Soyer

THE CAMPAIGN FOR DOMESTIC HAPPINESS ....Isabella Beeton

NOTES FROM MADRAS ....Colonel Wyvern

EXCITING FOOD FOR SOUTHERN TYPES ....Pellegrino Artusi

FROM ABSINTHE TO ZEST ....Alexandre Dumas

BUFFALO CAKE AND INDIAN PUDDING...................................Dr A. W. Chase

A LITTLE DINNER BEFORE THE PLAY ....Agnes Jekyll

MURDER IN THE KITCHEN ....Alice B. Toklas

LOVE IN A DISH & Other Pieces ....M. F. K. Fisher

A TASTE OF THE SUN ....Elizabeth David

A MIDDLE EASTERN FEAST...Claudia Roden

EATING WITH THE PILGRIMS & Other Pieces ....Calvin Trillin

RECIPES AND LESSONS FROM A DELICIOUS

   COOKING REVOLUTION ....Alice Waters